VOLLEYBALL DRILL BOOK

Game Action Drills

BOB BERTUCCI and JAMES PETERSON

MASTERS PRESS

NTC/Contemporary Publishing Group

Library of Congress Cataloging-in-Publication Data

Bertucci, Bob.
    Volleyball drill book: game action drills / Bob Bertucci and James Peterson.
       p.   cm.
    ISBN 0-940279-42-8
    1. Volleyball—Training.   I. Peterson, James A., 1943-   II. Title.
  GV1015.5.T73B49   1993
  796.325—dc20   92-33386
                                                         CIP

Rear cover photos provided by the University of Oregon Sports Information Office
and Pepperdine University Sports Information Office.
Front cover photograph by Nathaniel Butler.
All interior photos by Nathaniel Butler except those on page 1, provided by Purdue
University Sports Information Office, pages 93 and 189, provided by University of
Texas Sports Information Office, pages 111 and 129 provided by Ohio State
University Sports Information Office, and on page 167 provided by Tim Tessalone,
University of Southern California Sports Information Office.
Diagrams by Julie Biddle.

Published by Masters Press
A division of NTC/Contemporary Publishing Group, Inc.
4255 West Touhy Avenue, Lincolnwood (Chicago), Illinois 60712-1975 U.S.A.
Copyright © 1992 by Bob Bertucci
Printed in the United States of America
International Standard Book Number: 0-940279-42-8
00 01 02 03 04 05 RCP 22 21 20 19 18 17 16 15 14 13 12 11 10 9 8 7 6 5

INTRODUCTION

Volleyball Drill Book: Game Action Drills provides both coaches and teachers with a comprehensive tool for teaching volleyball skills and techniques to athletes. The emphasis is on teaching skills in a progressive manner in actual game action sequences and situations.

To fully benefit from the drills in this book, it is important to know how effective drills for skill development are designed. If you fully understand the process of designing a drill, you will be better prepared to use these drills to create your own drills to meet the needs of your team or class.

The basic structure of a drill is fairly straightforward. A drill should have an **objective** that relates to the activity. The objective should be realistic, accurate, and comprehensible to all participants. A drill should also involve training variables that can be manipulated to achieve the drill's objective. Four of the most common drill variables are *type*, *quantity*, *quality*, and *intensity*.

The *type* of drill involves several factors. For example, does the drill address the movement (static versus dynamic)? Does the drill focus on mechanics or technique? Does the drill incorporate a simulation of the skills or a game sequence involving the skill?

The *quantity* of a drill addresses the question of "how much?" Does the drill last for a specific length of time or until a specific number of contacts have been made?

The *quality* of a drill involves performing the drill until a predetermined level of achievement has been attained. For example, the drill is continued until the players are able to correctly execute a number of successful contacts or are able to demonstrate an certain level of proficiency in a particular task or skill.

The *intensity* of a drill can also be manipulated to achieve desired results. For example, by gradually decreasing the amount of time between contacts, you can progressively increase the level of intensity. You can also make a drill more physically demanding by increasing the number of contacts involved or the length of the drill.

How the variables are manipulated can have a profound effect on what the drill accomplishes. For example, the more dynamic movement involved in the drill (all other factors being equal), the more relevance it should have to the actual game. The more emphasis put on quality of performance in a high intensity drill, the more the drill enhances the ability to perform a skill while fatigued.

If you design a drill and it does not produce the expected results, you should review the design of the drill as it relates to following parameters:
1. The number of balls, nets, and special equipment needed.
2. The number of players needed in the drill.
   a) How many active learners?
   b) How many non-active learners (shaggers)?
3. Physical conditioning of the athletes.
4. Skill level of the athletes.
5. Mental and emotional level of the athletes.
   a) Level of concentration needed.
   b) Frustration and/or boredom factor.
   c) Is the drill oriented toward a specific skill, competitive, or game-like?

After a drill has been developed, it can be categorized in several ways. One of the most common methods for categorizing drills is as *coach-oriented* or *player-oriented* . In a coach-oriented drill, the coach is the center of the action. This enables the coach to manipulate training variables directly. Coach-oriented drills can be very effective for a skilled coach, especially if the players lack skills. However, a program that includes too many coach-oriented drills should be avoided, because such an approach reduces the role of the players. In player-oriented drills, the players perform the drills by themselves. The coach's primary duty is to teach and supervise.

A second popular way to categorize drills is by the difficulty and number of skills practiced within a drill. Drills can be divided by this method into three categories: *simple*, *combination*, and *complex*.

A simple drill is one repetition of one skill or multiple repetitions of one skill. Simple drills were addressed extensively in *Volleyball Drill Book: Individual Skills* and are very effective for teaching volleyball fundamentals. At higher levels of play and competition, simple drills should be used in pre-season training and as warm-up exercises.

Combination drills involve repetitions of two or more skills not in succession. These drills enable players to practice a number of different skills, and provide some degree of application to the game.

Complex drills, which are the focus of this text, involve repetitions of two or more skills performed in succession. As a rule, complex drills have the most application to the game and should always be designed with a game sequence in mind.

Finally, drills can be categorized by the number of participants involved in a drill: *individual drills*, *small group drills*, and *team drills*.

Understanding and incorporating all of these categories, variables, and considerations is important to developing a well- rounded training program. Keep in mind that variety is important to maximize the benefits of drills. As a result, your ability to select (and design) specific drills to meet specific needs can be a critical factor in preparing your team for game day.

Good luck in training your team. The drills presented in this book have been designed to maximize your team's level of success.

TABLE OF CONTENTS

VOLLEYBALL DRILL BOOK:
GAME ACTION DRILLS

KEY TO DIAGRAMS

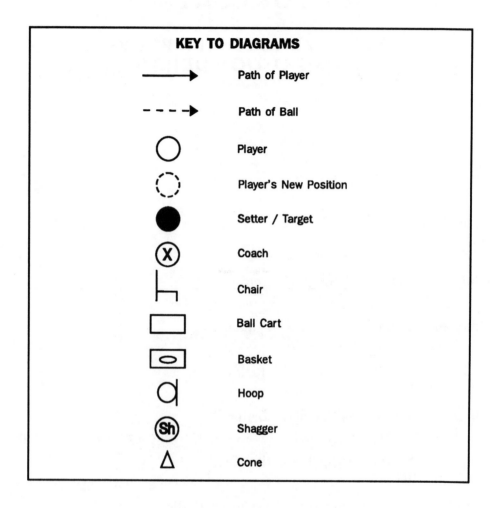

⟶	Path of Player
- - -►	Path of Ball
◯	Player
◌	Player's New Position
●	Setter / Target
Ⓧ	Coach
⊢	Chair
▭	Ball Cart
▭	Basket
◖	Hoop
Ⓢⓗ	Shagger
△	Cone

CHAPTER 1

INDIVIDUAL DIGGING CIRCUITS

1 DIG AND ROLL DRILL

Objective: To teach the skills involved in receiving spikes and executing emergency techniques.

Description: The drill begins when the coach spikes a ball to digger A. As soon as A passes the ball, the coach immediately tosses or spikes a second ball at A. Player A must play the ball with the correct execution of an emergency technique.

Variations:

1. Conduct the drill from all backcourt defensive positions.

2. Have the coach stand on a table and spike the ball at the diggers.

3. Have the coach use a variety of attack positions.

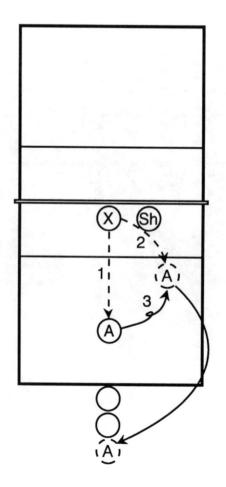

GAME ACTION DRILLS

2 PICK'EM ALL UP DRILL

Objective: To develop defensive reactions.

Description: The coach stands on a table and runs one player at a time through the following sequence. Start with a dig; pick up a tip; set a ball to the left (#4) front position; run a ball down, simulated spike off a block; dig a spike; pick up a tip. As soon as the first player in each group is finished, the next should be ready to go. Use groups of three's with each player going through five times.

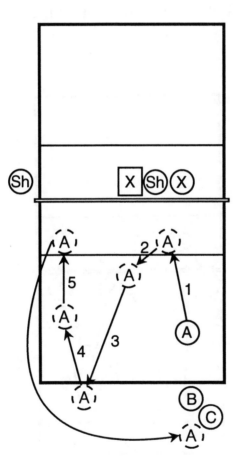

3 CONTROLLED CIRCUIT DRILL

Objective: To improve block recovery skills, digging, emergency techniques, and spiking.

Description: Player A begins the drill by mock blocking. On descent, player B throws the ball directly over and behind player A. Player A must recover from the block, step, and pass the ball to the coach. Then player A immediately moves to dig the same ball being passed by the coach to the left back (#5) position. Player A digs this ball back to the coach, who quickly spikes again to the right back (#1) position. A is still required to play the ball up, so that the coach can set the ball to the right front (#2) position. Player A finishes the circuit in the #2 position with a spike. This drill should require each player to make three successful trips through the circuit.

Variation: Run the drill from the other side of the net.

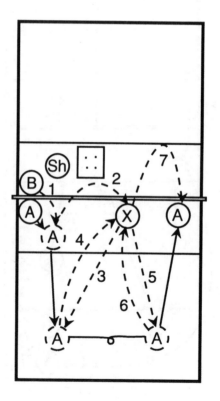

4 DIG, DIVE, AND DRIVE DRILL

Objective: To practice digging and emergency techniques, playing balls out of the net, and spiking transitions.

Description: The coach hits directly at the center back (#6) position for player A to dig. The coach then hits a ball to the right back (#1) position for a diving save and then hits a ball in front of player A so a sprawl or dive must be used. Player A then runs to the net and plays a ball out of the net on the same side of the court. Next the player back-pedals and makes three attacks on sets coming from a setter. Work the drill with groups of three's, with each player going through three times and then becoming a shagger.

Variations:

1. Vary sets to the hitter.

2. Run the same drill using digs without dives.

3. Add a block.

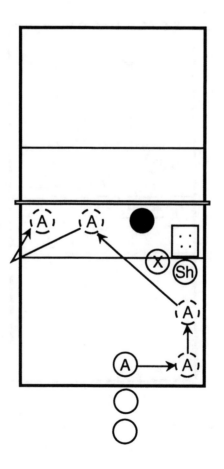

5 DEFENSIVE CIRCUIT DRILL

Objective: To train defensive play and movement.

Description: Player A blocks in the left front (#4) position. After blocking, player A turns and plays a tossed ball back to the coach. Then player A runs to the left back (#5) position, assumes the ready position, and digs two hard-driven spikes from a tosser. Next, player A runs to the right back (#1) position where a second tosser tosses a ball so that player A has to dive to play the ball. (At this time, player B starts at station #1.) Player A now moves to the right front (#2) position to hit a high ball tossed by the coach. After hitting, player A moves to the center and hits a "2" ball. As player A finishes with the attack, player A moves to the other side of the net to block player B's regular hit in position #2 and then blocks the "2" ball from the center front (#3) position.

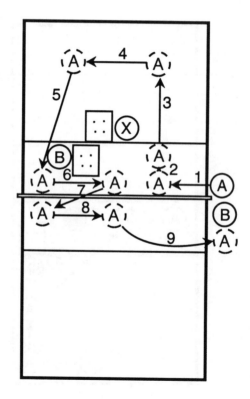

CHAPTER 2

THREE PLAYER PEPPER
SEQUENCES

6 THREE PERSON PEPPER DRILL

Objective: To practice the skills and sequence of dig, set, and spike.

Description: Player A begins the drill by setting to player B. Player B spins toward player C. Player C digs the ball to player A. The sequence is repeated for a prescribed number or amount of time. The players rotate one position.

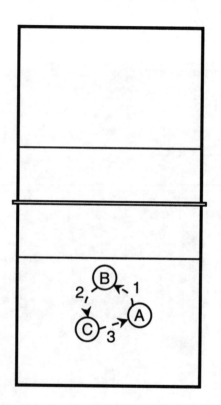

7 RIGHT TO RIGHT BACK PEPPER DRILL

Objective: To develop the skill of digging in the right back (#1) defensive position against a line attack.

Description: Player A begins the drill by setting to player B. Player B spikes the ball down the sideline toward player C who controls the dig to player A. The drill is repeated continuously.

Variation: Start the digging player at a base/starting position, and have this player adjust to the assigned defensive position in time to dig.

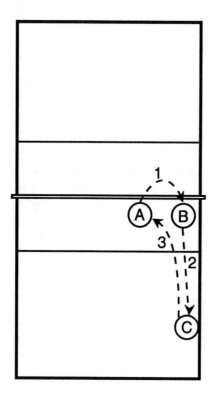

8 RIGHT TO MIDDLE BACK PEPPER DRILL

Objective: To develop the skill of digging in the middle back (#6) defensive position.

Description: Player A begins the drill by setting to player B. Player B spikes the ball deep to the middle toward player C. Player C controls the dig to player A. The drill is repeated continuously.

Variation: Start the digging player at a base/starting position, and have this player adjust to the assigned defensive position in time to dig.

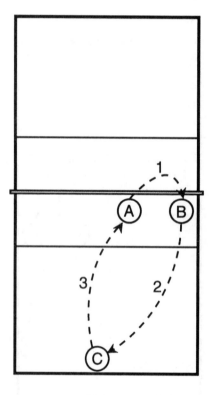

9 RIGHT TO LEFT BACK PEPPER DRILL

Objective: To develop the skill of digging in the left back (#5) defensive position against a cross-court attack.

Description: Player A begins the drill by setting to player B. Player B spikes the ball cross-court to the left back sideline toward player C. Player C controls the dig to player A. The drill is repeated continuously.

Variation: Start the digging player at a base/starting position, and have this player adjust to the assigned defensive position in time to dig.

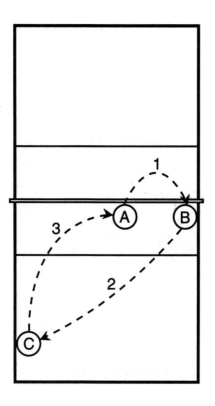

10 RIGHT FRONT PEPPER DRILL

Objective: To develop the skill of digging in the left front (#4) off blocking position.

Description: Player A begins the drill by setting to player B. B spikes the ball cross-court to the left front sideline around the attack line toward player C. Player C controls the dig to player A. The drill is repeated continuously.

Variation: Start the digging player at a base/starting position, and have this player adjust to the assigned defensive position in time to dig.

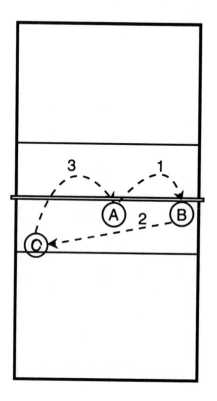

11 MIDDLE TO RIGHT BACK PEPPER DRILL

Objective: To develop the skill of digging in the right back (#1) defensive position against a middle attack.

Description: Player A begins the drill by setting to player B. B spikes the ball toward player C. Player C controls the dig to player A. The drill is repeated continuously.

Variation: Start the digging player at a base/starting position, and have this player adjust to the assigned defensive position in time to dig.

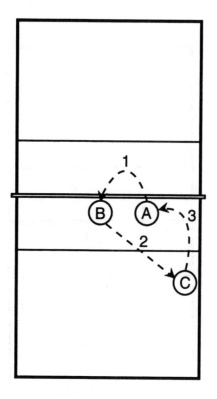

12 MIDDLE TO MIDDLE BACK PEPPER DRILL

Objective: To develop the skill of digging in the middle back (#6) defensive position against a middle attack.

Description: Player A begins the drill by setting to player B. Player B spikes the ball deep to the middle toward player C. Player C controls the dig to player A. The drill is repeated continuously.

Variation: Start the digging player at a base/starting position, and have this player adjust to the assigned defensive position in time to dig.

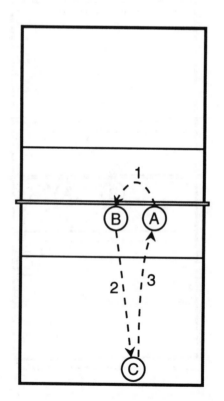

13 MIDDLE TO LEFT BACK PEPPER DRILL

Objective: To develop the skill of digging in the left back (#5) position against a middle attack.

Description: Player A begins the drill by setting to player B. Player B spikes the ball cross-court to the left back sideline toward player C. Player C controls the dig to player A. The drill is repeated continuously.

Variation: Start the digging player at a base/starting position, and have this player adjust to the assigned defensive position in time to dig.

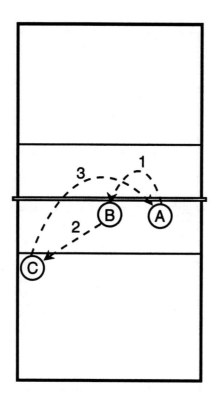

14 LEFT TO RIGHT BACK PEPPER DRILL

Objective: To develop the skill of digging in the right back (#1) position against a cross-court attack.

Description: Player A begins the drill by setting to player B. Player B spikes the ball cross-court to the right back sideline toward player C. Player C controls the dig to player A. The drill is repeated continuously.

Variation: Start the digging player at a base/starting position, and have this player adjust to the assigned defensive position in time to dig.

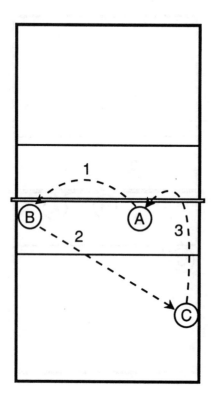

15 LEFT TO MIDDLE BACK PEPPER DRILL

Objective: To develop the skill of digging in the middle back (#6) defensive position.

Description: Player A begins the drill by setting to player B. Player B spikes the ball deep to the middle toward player C. Player C controls the dig to player A. The drill is repeated continuously.

Variation: Start the digging player at a base/starting position, and have this player adjust to the assigned defensive position in time to dig.

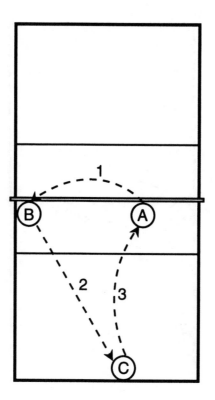

16 LEFT TO LEFT BACK PEPPER DRILL

Objective: To develop the skill of digging in the left back (#5) position against a line attack.

Description: Player A begins the drill by setting to player B. Player B spikes down the line toward player C. Player C controls the dig to player A. The drill is repeated continuously.

Variation: Start the digging player at a base/starting position, and have this player adjust to the assigned defensive position in time to dig.

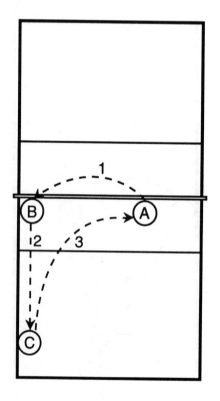

17 FOUR TO ONE PEPPER DRILL

Objective: To develop the skill of digging in the right back (#1) defensive position against a line attack.

Description: Player A begins the drill by setting over the net to player B. Player B spikes the ball down the sideline toward player C who controls the dig to player A. The drill is repeated continuously.

Variation: Start the digging player at a base/starting position, and have this player adjust to the assigned defensive position in time to dig.

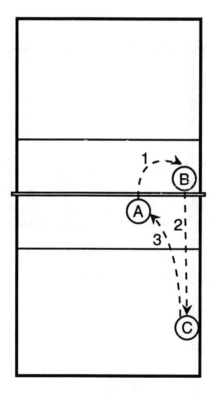

18 FOUR TO SIX PEPPER DRILL

Objective: To develop the skill of digging in the middle back (#6) defensive position.

Description: Player A begins the drill by setting over the net to player B. Player B spikes the ball deep to the middle toward player C. Player C controls the dig to player A. The drill is repeated continuously.

Variation: Start the digging player at a base/starting position, and have this player adjust to the assigned defensive position in time to dig.

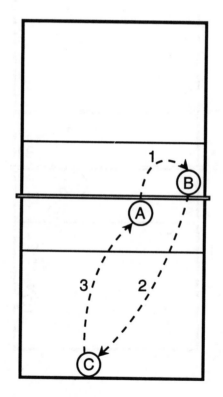

19 FOUR TO FIVE PEPPER DRILL

Objective: To develop the skill of digging in the left back (#5) defensive position against a cross-court attack.

Description: Player A begins the drill by setting over the net to player B. Player B spikes the ball cross-court to the left back side toward player C. Player C controls the dig to player A. The drill is repeated continuously.

Variation: Start the digging player at a base/starting position, and have this player adjust to the assigned defensive position in time to dig.

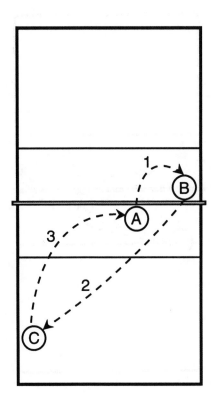

20 FOUR TO FOUR PEPPER DRILL

Objective: To develop the skill of digging in the left front (#4) off blocking position.

Description: Player A begins the drill by setting over the net to player B. Player B spikes the ball cross-court to the left front sideline around the attack line toward player C. Player C controls the dig to player A. The drill is repeated continuously.

Variation: Start the digging player at a base/starting position, and have this player adjust to the assigned defensive position in time to dig.

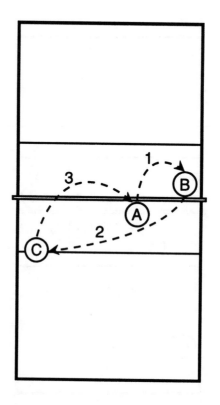

21 THREE TO ONE PEPPER DRILL

Objective: To develop the skill of digging in the right back (#1) defensive position against a middle attack.

Description: Player A begins the drill by setting over the net to player B. Player B spikes the ball toward player C. C controls the dig to player A. The drill is repeated continuously.

Variation: Start the digging player at a base/starting position, and have this player adjust to the assigned defensive position in time to dig.

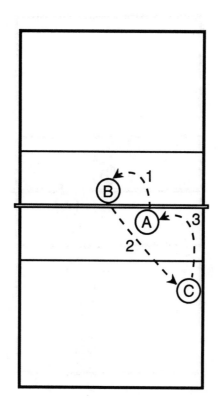

22 THREE TO THREE PEPPER DRILL

Objective: To develop the skill of digging in the middle back (#6) defensive position against a middle attack.

Description: Player A begins the drill by setting over the net to player B. Player B spikes the ball deep to the middle toward player C who controls the dig to player A. The drill is repeated continuously.

Variation: Start the digging player at a base/starting position, and have this player adjust to the assigned defensive position in time to dig.

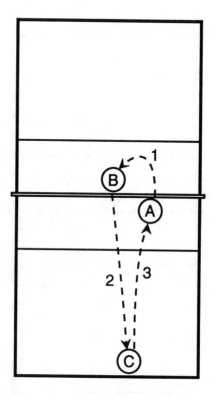

23 THREE TO FIVE PEPPER DRILL

Objective: To develop the skill of digging in the left back (#5) position against a middle attack.

Description: Player A begins the drill by setting over the net to Player B. Player B spikes the ball cross-court to the left back sideline toward player C. Player C controls the dig to player A. The drill is repeated continuously.

Variation: Start the digging player at a base/starting position, and have this player adjust to the assigned defensive position in time to dig.

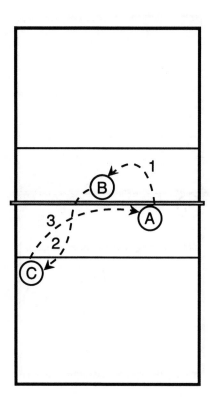

24 TWO TO ONE PEPPER DRILL

Objective: To train the skill of digging in the right back (#1) position against a cross-court attack.

Description: Player A begins the drill by setting over the net to player B. Player B spikes the ball cross-court to the right back sideline toward player C. Player C controls the dig to player A. The drill is repeated continuously.

Variation: Start the digging player at a base/starting position, and have this player adjust to the assigned defensive position in time to dig.

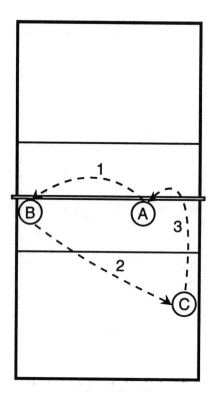

25 TWO TO THREE PEPPER DRILL

Objective: To train the skill of digging in the middle back (#6) defensive
position.

Description: Player A begins the drill by setting over the net to player
B. Player B spikes the ball deep to the middle toward player C. Player
C controls the dig to player A. The drill is repeated continuously.

Variation: Start the digging player at a base/starting position, and have
this player adjust to the assigned defensive position in time to dig.

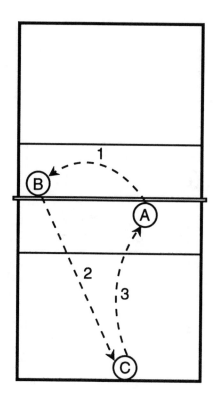

26 TWO TO FIVE PEPPER DRILL

Objective: To develop the skill of digging in the left back (#5) position against a line attack.

Description: Player A begins the drill by setting over the net to player B. Player B spikes the line toward player C. Player C controls the dig to player A. The drill is repeated continuously.

Variation: Start the digging player at a base/starting position, and have this player adjust to the assigned defensive position in time to dig.

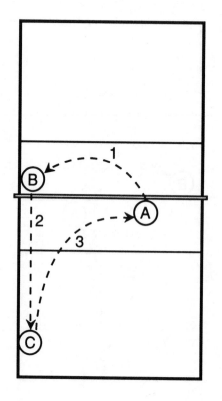

CHAPTER 3

DIG TRANSITION AND ATTACK SEQUENCES

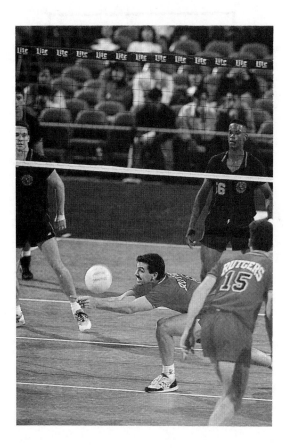

27 LEFT FRONT TRANSITION DRILL

Objective: To develop and train left front transition skills.

Description: Player A starts at the net. The coach slaps the ball, and
player A transitions for defense to receive the spike. Player A digs the
ball then transitions off to spike the ball. The coach tosses the ball, and
the player spikes it.

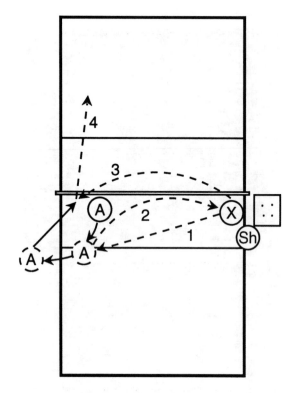

28 LEFT FRONT TRANSITION DRILL WITH SETTER

Objective: To develop and train left front transition off a set ball.

Description: Player A starts at the net. The coach slaps the ball, and player A transitions for defense to receive the spike. Player A digs the ball to the setter then transitions off to spike. The setter sets the ball, and player A approaches and spikes it.

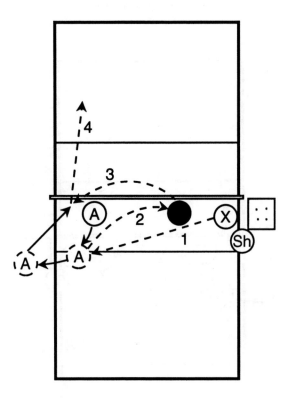

29 LEFT FRONT TRANSITION DRILL WITH PENETRATING SETTER

Objective: To develop and train left front transition with setter movement. To practice setting 2 "dug" balls.

Description: Player A starts at the net. The coach slaps the ball, and player A transitions for defense to receive the spike. Player A digs the ball to the target area then transitions off to spike the ball. The setter penetrates from the right back (#1) position and sets the ball to player A. Player A approaches and spikes the ball.

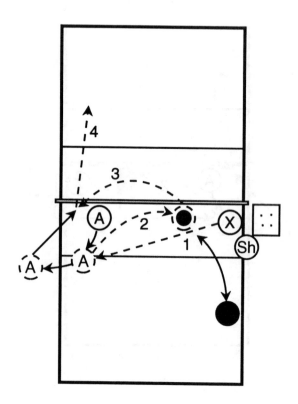

30 FOUR TO FOUR TRANSITION AND ATTACK DRILL

Objective: To train dropping off the net to dig, then transition to spiking sequence.

Description: Player A starts at the net. The coach slaps the ball, and player A transitions off the net for defense. The coach spikes the ball cross-court to the digger. Player A digs the ball to the setter and transitions off to spike. The setter sets outside, and player A approaches and spikes.

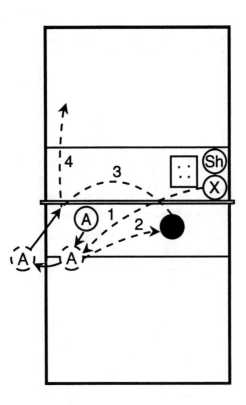

31 FOUR TO FOUR DIG TRANSITION AND ATTACK PROGRESSION DRILL

Objective: To practice dropping off the net to dig, then transition to attack sequence.

Description: The coach spikes a ball from a platform to player A after player A transitions from the net. Player A passes the ball to the target area and transitions out to spike. The setter sets a ball outside. Player A approaches and spikes.

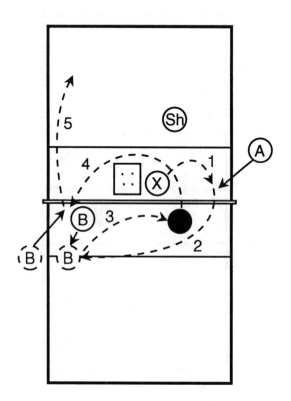

GAME ACTION DRILLS

32 FOUR TO FOUR TRANSITION AND ATTACK PROGRESSION DRILL WITH PENETRATING SETTER

Objective: To continue to train the progression of dig, transition and attack with a penetrating setter.

Description: Player A starts at the net. The coach is standing on a platform. The coach tosses the ball, and player A transitions off the net for defense. The coach spikes the ball cross-court toward player A. Player A digs the ball to the target area. The setter is penetrating to the area at the same time. Player A transitions to spike. The setter sets outside, and player A approaches and spikes.

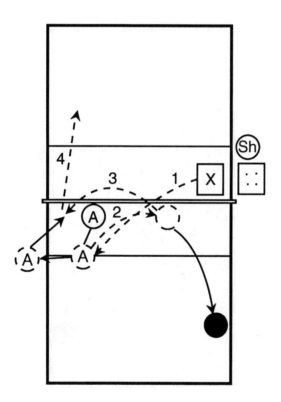

33 FOUR-FOUR TO THREE TRANSITION AND ATTACK DRILL

Objective: To train spikers transition from digging to attacking.

Description: Player A starts at the net in the left front (#4) position. The coach tosses the ball to spike, and player A transitions off into defensive position. The coach tips to the middle front (#3) position. Player A reacts to the tip to middle front area and plays the ball to the setter. Player A must immediately transition to a position from which an approach to spike can be accomplished. The setter sets the ball, and player A spikes.

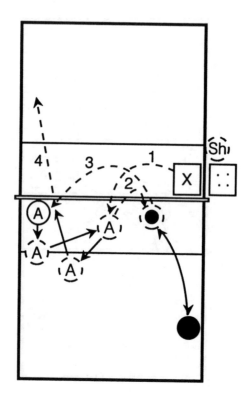

34 FOUR TO FOUR LIVE TRANSITION AND ATTACK DRILL

Objective: To continue to train digs, transitions, and attacks against an actual spiked ball.

Description: The coach tosses a ball to player A in the opposing left front (#4) position. Player A spikes the ball to the opposing left front (#4) position toward player B. Player B has already transitioned off the net and is prepared to dig player A. Player B digs the ball to the setter who sets the ball outside. Player A transitions outside, approaches, and spikes.

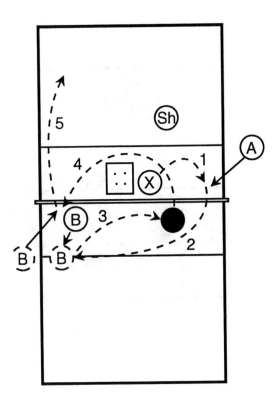

35 FOUR TO FOUR NON-STOP TRANSITION AND ATTACK DRILL

Objective: To practice game action dig, transition, and attack skills.

Description: The coach tosses one ball to the setter on the same side of the net. The setter sets to player A who hits a controlled shot to player B. Player B digs the ball to the setter and transitions to spike. The setter sets to player B. Player B approaches and spikes a controlled shot back to player A. The drill is continuously repeated.

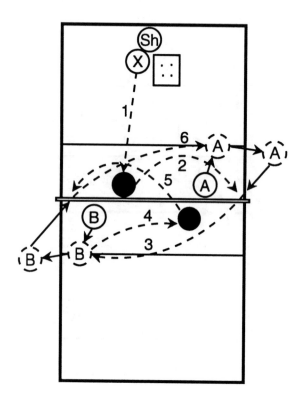

36 FOUR TO FOUR NON-STOP DRILL WITH PENETRATING SETTER

Objective: To develop setter penetration during game action while continuing to train dig, transition and attack.

Description: The coach tosses a ball to the setter who has just penetrated up to the net. The setter sets the ball to player A who hits a controlled shot to player B. As soon as player A spikes, the opposing setter penetrates to the target area. Player B digs the ball to the setter and transitions to spike. The setter sets to player B. Player B approaches and spikes a controlled shot back to player A. As either player spikes, one setter returns to original position after covering the spiker, while the other penetrates to the target area.

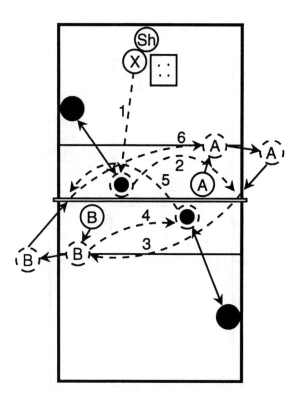

37 FOUR TO FOUR NON-STOP DRILL WITH BLOCKER

Objective: To teach the skill of digging around the block, while continuing to train dig, transition, and attack skills.

Description: The coach tosses a ball to the setter. The setter sets the ball for player A. Opposing player C blocks the line, channeling the ball to player B. Player A spikes the ball past player C toward player B. Player B has already dropped off the net to dig the ball to B's setter. Player B transitions to prepare to spike while the setter sets the ball outside. Player B spikes past blocker D to player A, and the drill continues.

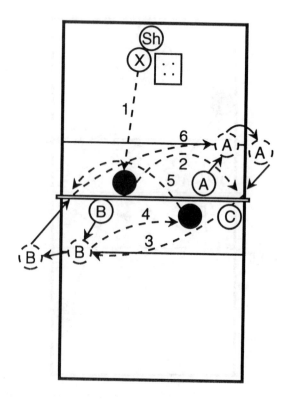

38 FOUR TO FOUR NON-STOP DRILL WITH BLOCKER AND PENETRATING SETTER

Objective: To teach the skill of digging around the block while continuing to train dig, transition, and attack skills.

Description: The coach tosses a ball to the setter that has just penetrated up to the net. The setter sets the ball for player A. Opposing player C blocks the line, channeling the ball to player B. Player A spikes the ball past player C toward player B. The setter on the opposite side of the net penetrates to the target area while player B drops off the net to dig the ball to the setter. Player B transitions to prepare to spike while the setter sets the ball outside. Player B spikes past blocker D to player A. The setter on the spiking side immediately returns to the starting position, while the opposing setter penetrates to continue the drill.

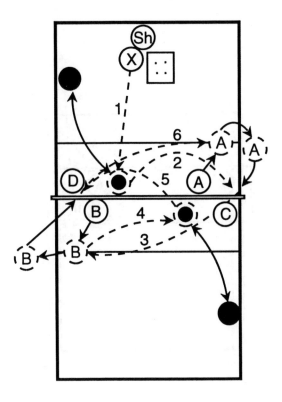

39 RIGHT FRONT TRANSITION DRILL

Objective: To develop and train right front transition skills and develop directional spiking skills.

Description: Player A starts at the net. The coach slaps the ball, and player A transitions for defense to receive the spike. The coach spikes the ball. Player A digs the ball to the target area then transitions off to spike the ball. The coach tosses the ball, and player A spikes it.

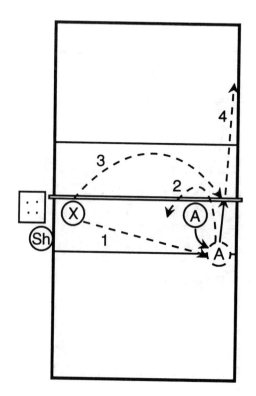

40 RIGHT FRONT TRANSITION DRILL WITH SETTER

Objective: To develop and train right front transition skills and develop directional spiking skills from a set ball.

Description: Player A starts at the net. The coach slaps the ball, and player A transitions for defense to receive the spike. The coach spikes the ball. Player A digs the ball to the setter then transitions off to spike the ball. The setter sets the ball, and player A approaches and spikes the ball.

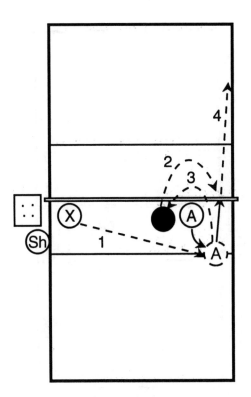

41 RIGHT FRONT TRANSITION DRILL WITH PENETRATING SETTER

Objective: To develop and train right front transition skills and develop directional spiking skills.

Description: Player A starts at the net. The coach slaps the ball, and player A transitions for defense to receive the spike. Player A digs the ball to the target area then transitions off to spike the ball. The setter penetrating from the right back (#1) position sets, and player A approaches the ball and spikes it.

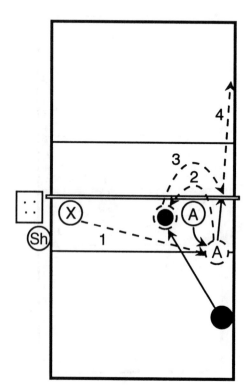

42 TWO TO TWO TRANSITION AND ATTACK DRILL

Objective: To train dropping off the net to dig, then transition to attack sequence.

Description: Player A starts at the net. The coach slaps the ball, and player A transitions off the net for defense. The coach spikes the ball cross-court to the digger. Player A digs the ball to the setter and transitions off to spike. The setter back sets, and player A approaches and spikes.

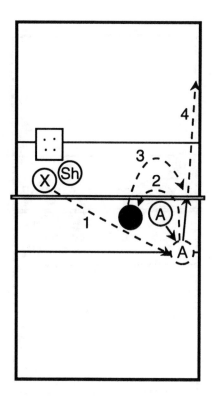

43 TWO TO TWO TRANSITION AND ATTACK PROGRESSION DRILL

Objective: To continue training dropping off the net to dig, then transition to attack sequence. To train directional spiking.

Description: The coach spikes a ball from a platform to player A after A transitions from the net. Player A passes the ball to the target area and transitions to spike. The setter back sets to player A outside. Player A approaches and spikes to a specified position on the court.

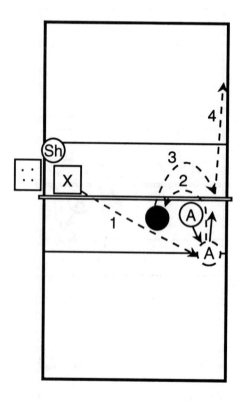

44 TWO TO TWO TRANSITION AND ATTACK PROGRESSION DRILL WITH PENETRATING SETTER

Objective: To continue to train the progression to dig, transition, attack from the right front with a penetrating setter.

Description: Player A starts at the net. The coach is standing on a platform on the opposite side of the net. The coach tosses the ball, and player A transitions off the net for defense. The coach spikes the ball cross-court to player A. Player A digs the ball to the target area as the setter transitions to the target area. Player A transitions to spike. The setter back sets, and player A approaches and spikes.

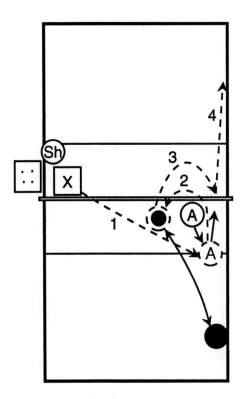

45 TRANSITION AND ATTACK TWO-TWO TO THREE DRILL

Objective: To train spiker's transition from digging to attacking.

Description: Player A starts at the net in the right front (#2) position. The coach tosses the ball to spike while player A transitions off into defensive position. The coach tips to the middle front (#3) position, and player A reacts to the tip and plays the ball up to the setter. Player A must immediately transition to a position from which an approach to spike can be accomplished. The setter back sets the ball, and player A spikes.

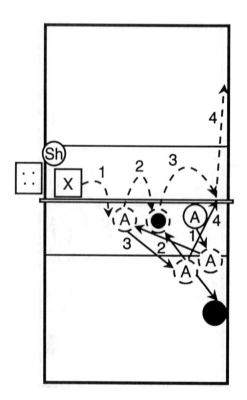

46 TWO TO TWO LIVE TRANSITION AND ATTACK DRILL

Objective: To continue to train dig transition attack skills against an actual spiked ball.

Description: The coach tosses a ball to player B in the opposing right front (#2) position. Player B spikes the ball to the opposing right front (#2) position toward player A. Player A has already transitioned off the net and is prepared to dig player B. Player A digs the ball to the setter who back sets the ball. Player A transitions, approaches, and spikes.

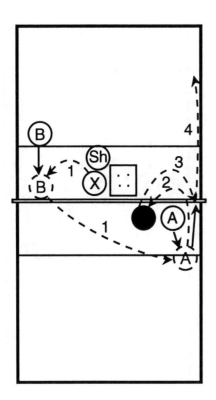

47 TWO TO TWO NON-STOP TRANSITION AND ATTACK DRILL

Objective: To improve game action dig, transition, and attack skills.

Description: The coach tosses one ball to a setter. The setter back sets to player A who hits a controlled shot to player B. Player B digs the ball to the setter and transitions to spike. The setter back sets to player B. Player B approaches and spikes a controlled shot to player A. The drill is continuously repeated.

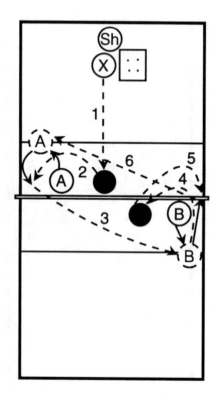

48 TWO TO TWO NON-STOP DRILL WITH PENETRATING SETTER

Objective: To develop setter penetration during game action while continuing to train dig, transition, and attack skills.

Description: The coach tosses a ball to the setter who has just penetrated up to the net. The setter back sets the ball to player A who hits a controlled shot to player B. As soon as player A spikes, the opposing setter penetrates to the target area. Player B digs the ball to the setter and transitions to spike. The setter back sets to player B. Player B approaches and spikes a controlled shot back to player A. As either player spikes, one setter returns to their original position, and the other setter penetrates to the target area.

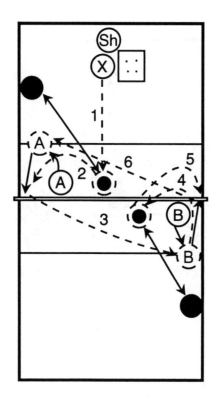

49 TWO TO TWO NON-STOP DRILL WITH BLOCKER

Objective: To teach digging around the block while continuing to train dig, transition, and attack skills.

Description: The coach tosses a ball to the setter. The setter back sets the ball for player A. Opposing player C blocks the line, channeling the ball to player B. Player A spikes the ball past player C toward player B. Player B has already dropped off the net to dig the ball to B's setter. Player B transitions to prepare to spike, while the setter back sets the ball. Player B spikes past blocker D to player A, and the drill continues.

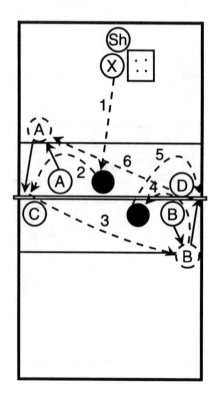

50 TWO TO TWO NON-STOP DRILL WITH BLOCKER AND PENETRATING SETTER

Objective: To teach digging around the block while continuing to train dig, transition, and attack skills.

Description: The coach tosses a ball to the setter who has just penetrated up to the net. The setter back sets the ball for player A. Opposing player C blocks the line, channeling the ball to player B. Player A spikes the ball past player C toward player B. The setter on the opposite side of the net penetrates to the target area, and player B drops off the net to dig the ball to the setter. Player B transitions to prepare to spike while the setter back sets the ball. Player B spikes past blocker D to player A. The drill continues. The setter on the spiking side immediately returns to the starting position, while the opposing setter penetrates to continue the drill.

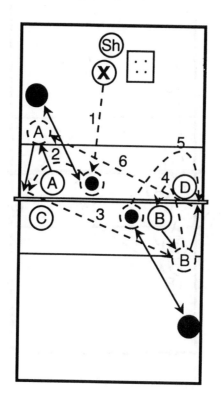

51 LEFT SIDE DEFENSE AND TRANSITION DRILL

Objective: To develop and train proper positioning and teamwork between the left front and left side defenders. To continue training for left front transition.

Description: Player A starts at the net, and player B starts near the attack line. The coach tosses the ball, and players A and B transition to their defensive positions. The coach spikes the ball toward player B. B digs the ball. Immediately after the dig, player A transitions to spike the ball. The coach tosses a second ball, and player A spikes it.

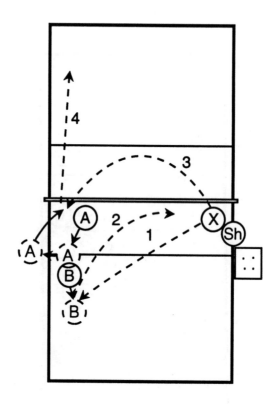

52 LEFT SIDE DEFENSE AND TRANSITION DRILL WITH SETTER

Objective: To continue to develop and train proper positioning and team-work between left side diggers. To continue training for left front transition.

Description: Players A and B assume their base or starting defensive positions. When the coach tosses the ball, players A and B transition to their new defensive positions. The coach spikes the ball toward their left side area of coverage. The appropriate player should dig the ball to the setter. Immediately after the dig, player A transitions to spike the ball. The setter sets outside to player A who approaches and spikes.

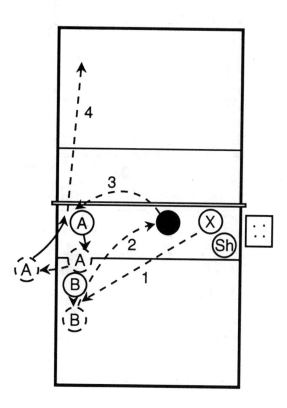

53 LEFT SIDE DEFENSE AND TRANSITION DRILL WITH PENETRATING SETTER

Objective: To train proper defensive positioning, teamwork, and transition to attack. To practice penetrating and setting a "dug" ball.

Description: The coach tosses the ball and hits at either digger. The digger digs to the target area in the middle or right third of the court along the net. Player A then transitions to spike as the setter penetrates to the net and sets to the left front (#4) position. Player A approaches and spikes the ball.

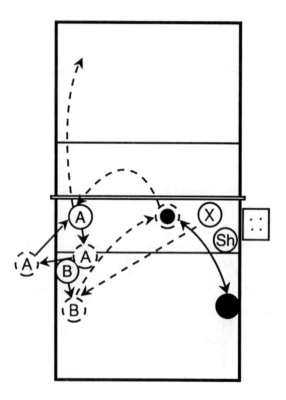

54 FOUR TO FOUR-FIVE DEFENSE AND TRANSITION DRILL WITH SETTER

Objective: To train left side defense and transition.

Description: The coach starts the drill by spiking the ball over the net to the left front digger. Player A digs the ball to the setter and transitions off to spike. The ball is set outside, and player A approaches and spikes. Players A and B assume starting positions immediately. The coach spikes another ball to player B, and the drill continues.

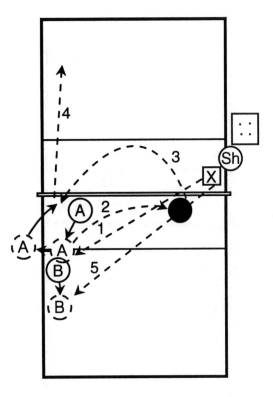

55 FOUR TO FOUR-FIVE DEFENSE AND TRANSITION DRILL WITH BLOCKING SETTER

Objective: To train proper defensive positioning, teamwork, and transition to attack.

Description: The coach spikes the ball around the blocker toward either defensive player A or B. (The coach should occasionally spike into the block to keep effort at high intensity.) The defensive player (B) digs the ball back to the target area. Player C recovers from blocking and sets to player A in the left front (#4) position. Player A transitions and approaches to spike the ball.

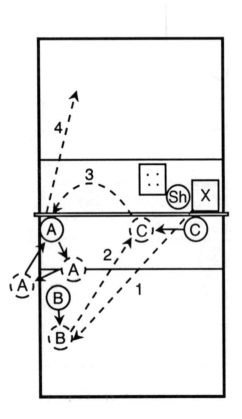

56 FOUR TO FOUR-FIVE DEFENSE AND TRANSITION DRILL WITH PENETRATING SETTER.

Objective: To train proper defensive positioning, teamwork, and transition to attack. To practice penetrating and setting a dug ball.

Description: The coach tosses the ball and spikes over the net at either digger. The diggers have transitioned from their starting positions to an adjusted defensive position. The digger digs to the target, and the setter penetrates to the net to set to the left front (#4) position. Player A, after the dig, transitions and approaches to spike the ball.

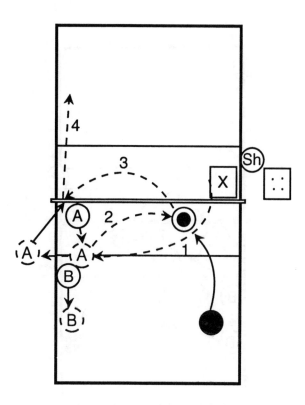

57 FOUR TO THREE VERSUS FOUR TO FIVE DEFENSE AND TRANSITION DRILL WITH PENETRATING SETTER

Objective: To train spiker transition from digging to attacking, and teamwork in defensive coverage. To continue training setter penetration and setting a dug ball.

Description: Players A and B start in their defensive base positions. The coach tosses the ball while both players transition to the appropriate defensive position. The coach tips to the middle front (#3) position area. Players A and B react to the tip. Depending on the location of the tip, the appropriate player plays the ball to the setter. Player A immediately transitions to a position from which an approach to spike can be accomplished. The setter sets the ball to player A.

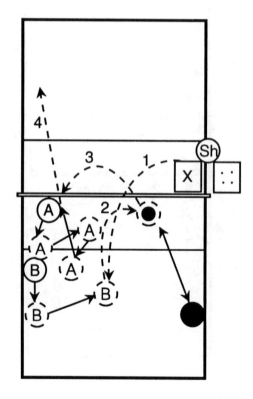

58 FOUR TO FOUR-FIVE LIVE TRANSITION AND ATTACK DRILL

Objective: A continued progression of dig, attack, and transition against an actual spiked ball.

Description: The coach tosses the ball to player A in the opposing left front (#4) position. Player A spikes the ball to the opposing left side digger, player B or C. Players B and C have already transitioned from their starting positions and are prepared to dig. In this case, player B digs the ball to the setter. The setter sets the ball outside, and player B transitions outside, approaches, and attacks.

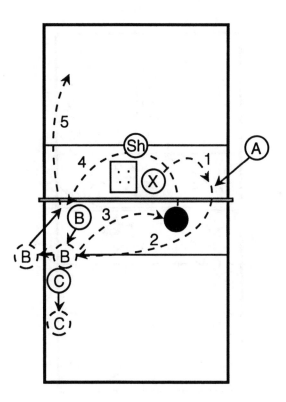

59 FOUR TO FOUR-FIVE NON-STOP TRANSITION AND ATTACK DRILL

Objective: To train game action defense, transition, and attack skills.

Description: The coach tosses one ball to the setter on the same side of the net. The setter sets to player A who spikes a controlled ball toward the opposing cross-court sideline. The appropriate digger digs the ball. In this diagram, player D digs the ball to the setter. Players A and B assume their starting positions while player C transitions to spike. The setter sets the ball outside to player C. Players A and B transition to dig a cross-court spike. Player C approaches and spikes a controlled ball cross-court toward player A or B.

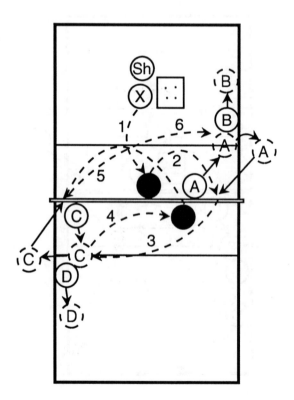

60 FOUR TO FOUR-FIVE NON-STOP DRILL WITH PENETRATING SETTER

Objective: To develop setter penetration during game action while continuing to train cross-court defense transaction and attack skills.

Description: The coach tosses a ball to the setter on the same side that has just penetrated up to the net. The setter sets the ball to player A who hits a controlled shot cross-court toward players C and D. As soon as player A spikes, the opposing setter penetrates to the target area. Either player C or D is prepared to dig. In this diagram, player D digs the ball to the setter and transitions to spike. The setter sets to player C. Player C approaches and spikes a controlled shot cross-court to either player A or B. As either player spikes, one setter returns to the original position after covering the spiker, and the other penetrates to the target area.

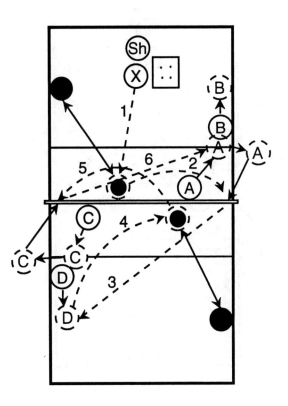

61 FOUR TO FOUR-FIVE NON-STOP DRILL WITH BLOCKER

Objective: To teach digging around the block while continuing to train defensive teamwork, transition, and attack skills.

Description: The coach tosses a ball to the setter. The setter sets the ball for player A. Opposing player C blocks the line, channeling the ball toward players D and E. Player A spikes the ball past player C toward players D and E. Players D and E have transitioned from their base positions to dig the cross-court spike to their setter. Player D transitions to prepare to spike while the setter sets the ball outside. Player D approaches and spikes past blocker F toward either player A or B, and the drill continues.

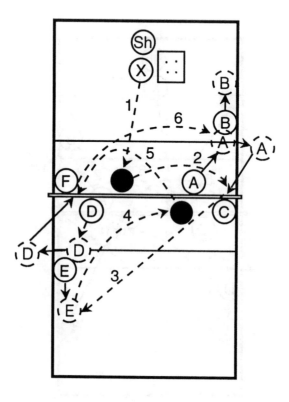

62 FOUR TO FOUR-FIVE NON-STOP DRILL WITH TWO BLOCKERS

Objective: To teach digging around the block while continuing to train defensive teamwork, transition, and attack skills.

Description: The coach tosses a ball to the setter. The setter sets the ball for player A. Opposing blockers, players C and D, block the line, channeling the ball toward players E and F. Player A spikes the ball past players C and D toward players E and F. E and F have transitioned from their base positions to dig the cross-court spike to their setter. Player E transitions to prepare to spike while the setter sets the ball outside. Player E approaches and spikes past blockers G and H toward either player A or B, and the drill continues.

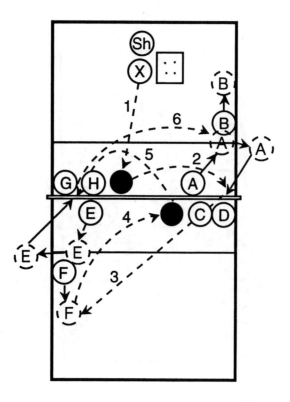

63 FOUR TO FOUR-FIVE NON-STOP DRILL WITH TWO BLOCKERS AND A PENETRATING SETTER

Objective: To teach digging around the block while continuing to train defensive teamwork, transition, and attack skills.

Description: The coach tosses a ball to the setter who has just penetrated to the net. The setter sets the ball for player A. The opposing blockers, players C and D, block the line, channeling the ball to players E and F. Player A spikes the ball past players C and D to players E and F. The setter on the opposite side of the net penetrates to the target area, and players E and F transition from their base positions to dig the cross-court spike to their setter. Player E transitions to prepare to spike while the setter sets the ball outside. Player E approaches and spikes past blockers G and H toward either player A or B. The setter on the spiking side immediately returns to the starting position while the opposing setter penetrates to continue the drill.

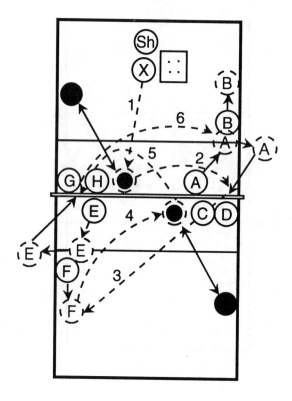

64 RIGHT SIDE DEFENSE AND TRANSITION DRILL

Objective: To develop and train proper positioning and teamwork between the right side defenders.

Description: Player A starts at the net, and player B starts near the attack line. The coach tosses the ball, and both players A and B transition for defense to receive the spike. Player A or B, depending on the location of the spike, digs the ball then transitions off to spike the ball. The coach tosses the ball, and the player approaches and spikes it.

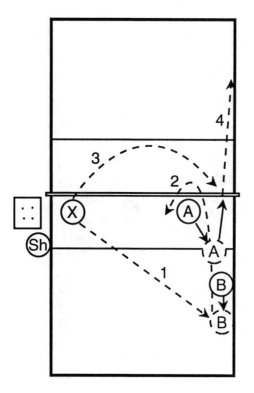

65 LEFT SIDE DEFENSE AND TRANSITION DRILL WITH SETTER

Objective: To develop and train the right side defensive transition and develop the directional spike.

Description: Players A and B assume their base or starting positions. The coach tosses the ball, and players A and B transition for defense to receive the spike. Player A or B, depending on the location of the spike, digs the ball to the setter then transitions off to spike the ball. The setter sets the ball, and the player approaches and spikes the ball.

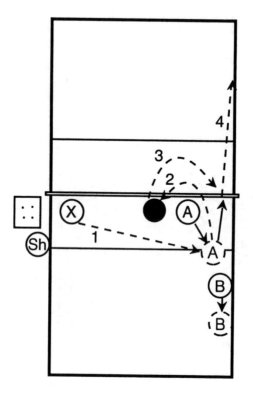

66 RIGHT SIDE DEFENSE AND TRANSITION DRILL

Objective: To develop and train right side defense, teamwork, and transition.

Description: Players A and B assume a starting or base position for defense. The coach tosses the ball, and players A and B transition for defense to receive a cross-court spike. Player B digs the ball to the target area, requiring player A to penetrate to set. Player A then sets the ball to the coach or to the attack line, and player B spikes from the backcourt. In the event that player A has to dig the next cross-court spike, player B will penetrate to the target area and back set the ball for player A to spike.

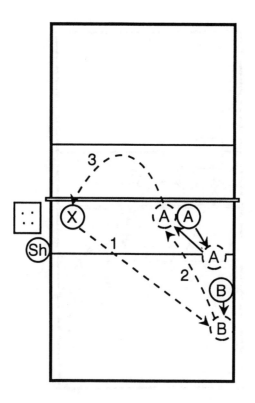

67 TWO TO TWO-ONE DEFENSE AND TRANSITION DRILL

Objective: To train right side defense, teamwork, and transition.

Description: Players A and B assume a starting or base position for defense. The coach tosses the ball, and players A and B transition into defensive position for a cross-court spike. The coach can spike to either player A or B. As shown in the diagram, player B digs the spiked ball to the target area. This requires player A to penetrate and set. Player A sets the ball to the coach or sets near the attack line for player B to spike from the backcourt. In the event that player A has to dig the next cross-court spike, player B will penetrate to the target area and back set the ball to player A to spike.

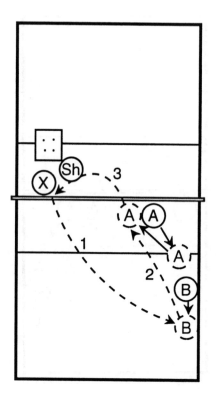

68 TWO TO TWO-ONE DEFENSE AND TRANSITION DRILL WITH BLOCKING SETTER

Objective: To train proper defensive positioning around a blocker. To develop teamwork and transition to attack skills.

Description: The coach spikes the ball around the blockers toward either defensive player A or B. As shown in the diagram, player A digs the ball to the target area, and player B penetrates to back set the ball to player A. Player A approaches and spikes the ball to a specific location. In the event that player B digs the ball, player A penetrates to the target area and sets a ball for player B to execute a back court attack.

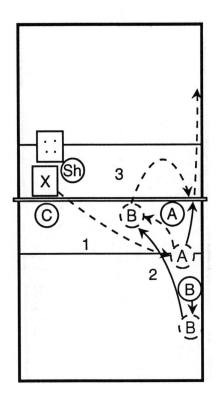

69 TWO TO THREE VERSUS ONE TO TWO DEFENSE AND TRANSITION DRILL

Objective: To train teamwork in right side defense and transition.

Description: Players A and B assume a starting or base position for defense. The coach begins the drill by tossing a ball to spike, and players A and B transition for defense against a cross-court spike. The coach tips the ball deep toward the center of the court. Player B digs the ball to the target area, requiring player A to penetrate to set. Player A then sets the ball to the coach or near the attack line for B to spike from the back court. In the event that player A digs the next cross-court tip or spike, player B will penetrate to the target area and back set the ball to player A to spike.

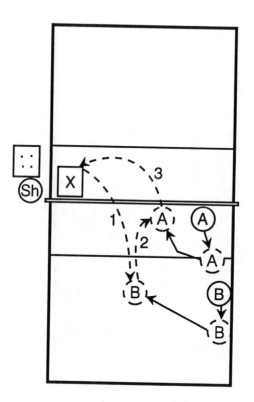

70 TWO TO TWO-ONE LIVE RIGHT SIDE DEFENSE AND TRANSITION DRILL

Objective: To train right side defense against a live attack, teamwork, and transition.

Description: Player A and B assume a starting or base position for defense. The coach tosses a ball to player C on the opposite side of the net. Player C spikes cross-court to either player A or B who have transitioned into their defensive positions. As shown in the diagram, player C spikes to player B who digs to the target area. Player A must penetrate to set. Player A then sets the ball to player C, and the drill continues. Player may also set for a backcourt attack by player B. B spikes to player C as shown above. In the event that player A digs the next cross-court spike, player B will penetrate to the target area and back set the ball to player A to spike.

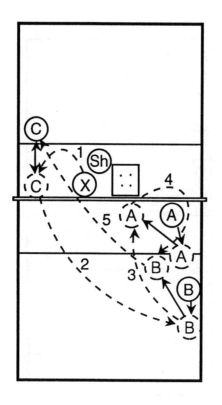

71 TWO TO TWO-ONE NON-STOP RIGHT SIDE DEFENSE AND TRANSITION DRILL

Objective: To continue the training progression for right side defense, teamwork, transition, and ball control.

Description: The coach tosses a ball to player D, the setter on the same side of the court, who has just penetrated up to the net. Player D back sets the ball to player C. As soon as the ball is set, players A and B transition from a base position to prepare for a cross-court attack. Player C approaches and spikes to either A or B. As shown in the above diagram, player C spikes to player B who digs to the target area. Player A must penetrate to set. Player A then sets a backcourt attack to player B who spikes to either player C or player D on the opposing side. In the event that player A or C digs during the drill, player B or D would penetrate to the target area and back set to player A or C.

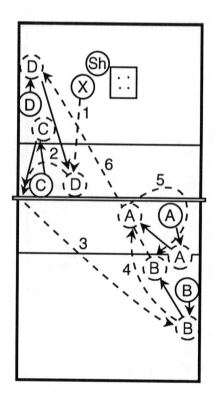

72 TWO TO TWO-ONE NON-STOP DRILL WITH BLOCKER

Objective: To train right side defense around one blocker and develop transition skills and ball control.

Description: The coach tosses a ball to player D, the setter on the same side of the court, who has just penetrated up to the net. Player D back sets the ball to player C. As soon as the ball is set, players A and B transition from their basic positions to prepare for a cross-court attack. Player C approaches and must spike the ball past the line blocker, player E, cross-court to either player A or B. As shown in the diagram, Player C spikes to player B who digs to the target area, requiring player A to penetrate to set. Player A then sets for a backcourt attack to player B who must spike past blocker F. Player B may spike to either player C or D. In the event that player A or C dig during the drill, player B or D would penetrate to the target area and execute a normal back set to players A and C.

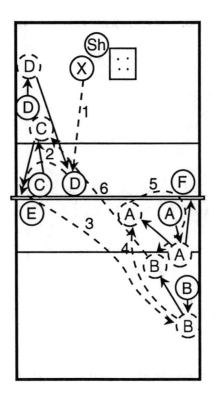

Dig Transition and Attack Sequences

73 TWO TO TWO-ONE NON-STOP DRILL WITH TWO BLOCKERS

Objective: To train the right side defense around two blockers, transitions, and ball control.

Description: The coach tosses a ball to player D, the setter on the same side of the court, who has just penetrated to the net. Player D back sets the ball to player C. As soon as the ball is set, players A and B transition from the base position to prepare for a cross-court attack. Player C approaches and must spike the ball past the line blockers, E and F, cross-court to either player A or B. As shown, player C spikes to player B who digs to the target area, requiring player A to penetrate to set. Player A then sets for a back court attack to player B who must spike past players G and H blocking the line. Player B may spike to either player C or D. In the event that player A or C digs during the drill, player B or D would penetrate to the target area and execute a normal back set to players A or C.

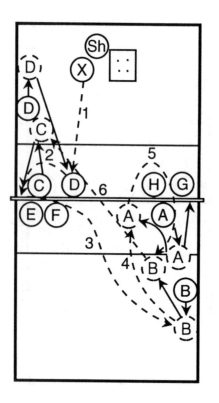

74 ONE TO FOUR DEFENSE, TRANSITION, AND ATTACK DRILL

Objective: To develop continuity of digging, setting, and hitting. To train positioning and transitioning for attack.

Description: The drill begins with the coach tossing the ball and players A and B transitioning out of their starting or base positions. The coach spikes at either player A or B who digs to the setter. The setter must get to the ball and set it to player B. Player B transitions, approaches, and spikes the ball. The players immediately return to their starting positions. The coach tosses the ball and the drill continues.

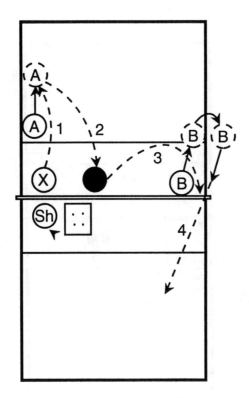

75 FOUR TO ONE-FOUR DEFENSE, TRANSITION, AND ATTACK DRILL

Objective: To practice digging, setting, and hitting. To develop teamwork, and transition to attack abilities.

Description: The drill begins with the coach tossing the ball and players A and B transitioning out of their starting or base positions. The coach spikes the ball at player A who digs to the setter. The setter sets to the left front (#4) position to player B. Player B transitions to attack immediately after player A digs. The setter sets to player B who approaches and attacks. As soon as the ball is spiked, the coach tosses the next ball. Players stay in the same group until the coach has them rotate.

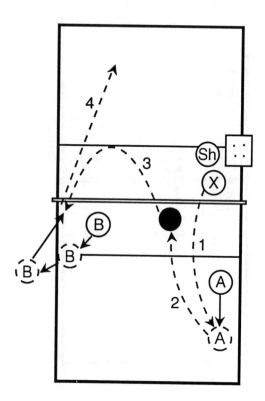

76 FOUR TO ONE-FOUR DEFENSE, TRANSITION, AND ATTACK PROGRESSION DRILL

Objective: To train digging, setting, and hitting skills. To develop defensive positioning and transition to attack.

Description: The drill begins with the coach tossing the ball and players A and B transitioning out of their starting or base positions. The coach spikes the ball at either player A or B who digs to the setter. The setter sets to the left front (#4) position to player B. Player B transitions to attack immediately after player A digs the ball. The setter sets, and player B approaches and attacks.

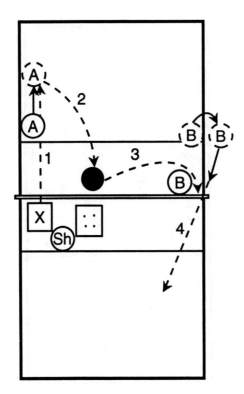

77 FOUR TO THREE-TWO VERSUS ONE TO FOUR DEFENSE, TRANSITION, AND ATTACK DRILL

Objective: To train tip coverage and transition to attack.

Description: The drill begins with the coach tossing the ball and players A and B transitioning from their base positions. The coach mixes spikes and tips toward center front (#3) and right front (#2) positions. Both players move to play the tipped or spiked balls. The appropriate player should play the ball to the setter, and player B must transition to spike. The setter sets to player B in the left front (#4) position. Player B approaches and attacks, and the drill continues.

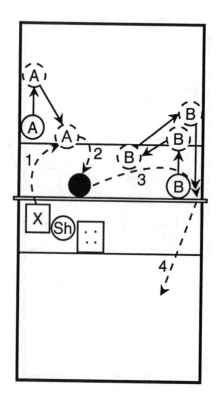

78 FOUR TO ONE-FOUR LIVE DEFENSE, TRANSITION, AND ATTACK DRILL

Objective: To train defense, transition, and attack against an actual spiked ball.

Description: The drill begins with the coach tossing the ball to player C who approaches and spikes to either player A or B. As shown below, player C elected to spike to player A. Player A digs to the setter in the target area. Once the spike was made toward player A, player B transitions to prepare to spike. The setter sets to player B in the left front (#4) position. Player B approaches and spikes to a specific pre-determined area. The coach tosses another ball and the drill continues.

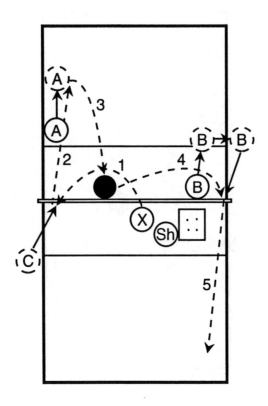

79 FOUR TO ONE-FOUR NON-STOP TRANSITION AND ATTACK DRILL

Objective: To develop game action dig, transition, and attack skills.

Description: The drill begins when the coach tosses the ball to the setter. The setter sets to player C. Both players A and B transition from their starting positions to their new defensive positions and prepare to dig. Player C approaches and spikes the ball down the line to player A. Player A digs the ball to the setter on the same side of the net. Player B transitions to attack. The setter sets the ball to player B who approaches and spikes to player C. C digs the ball to the setter, and the drill continues. In the second sequence, player C should spike cross-court to player B and player A to player D.

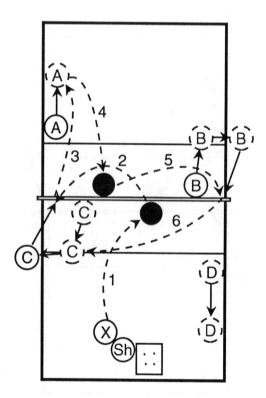

80 FOUR TO ONE-FOUR NON-STOP DRILL WITH BLOCKER

Objective: To teach digging around the block while continuing to train dig, transition, and attack skills.

Description: The drill begins with the coach tossing the ball to the setter. The setter sets the ball to player C. Both players A and B transition from their starting position to a new defensive position and prepare to dig. Player C approaches and spikes the ball past player F toward player A. Player A digs the ball to player F who, after jumping to block, transitions to the target area, prepares to set. Player B transitions to attack, and player F sets to the left front (#4) position. Player B approaches and spikes the ball cross-court past blocker E to player C. Player C digs the ball to the target area. Player E transitions to set in the target area after landing from blocking. Player C transitions to attack and player E sets the ball to the left front (#4) position. Player C approaches and now spikes past the block cross-court to player B, alternating the direction of the spike and the digger.

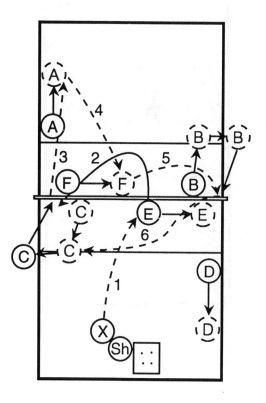

81 TWO TO FIVE DEFENSE, TRANSITION, AND ATTACK DRILL

Objective: To develop continuity in digging, setting, and hitting. To train positioning and transitioning for attack.

Description: The coach tosses a ball to spike while players A and B move from a starting position to a new defensive position. The coach spikes at either player A or B. The player digs to the setter. The setter must get to the ball and back set it to player A. Player A transitions, approaches, and spikes the ball. The players immediately return to their starting positions. The coach tosses the ball, and the drill continues.

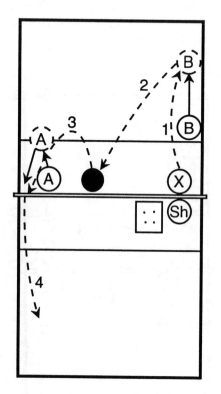

82 TWO TO TWO-FIVE DEFENSE, TRANSITION, AND ATTACK DRILL

Objective: To practice digging, setting, and hitting skills. To develop teamwork and transition to attack.

Description: The coach spikes the ball to either player A or B who digs the ball to the setter. In this diagram, the coach spikes to player B. The setter back sets to the right front (#2) position to player A. Player A transitions to attack immediately after player B digs the ball. The setter back sets to player A who approaches and attacks. As soon as the ball is spiked, the coach tosses the next ball and the drill continues.

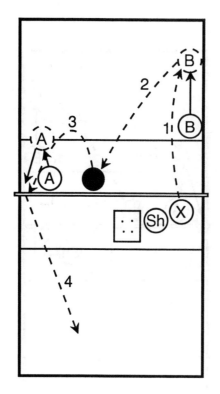

83 TWO TO TWO-FIVE DEFENSE, TRANSITION, AND ATTACK PROGRESSION DRILL

Objective: To train digging, setting, and hitting skills. To develop a player's defensive positioning and transition to attack.

Description: The drill begins with the coach tossing the ball and players A and B transitioning out of their starting or base positions. The coach spikes the ball at either player A or B. The player digs to the setter. The setter back sets to the right front (#2) position to player A. Player A transitions to attack immediately after player B digs the ball. After A spikes, the coach tosses again, and the drill repeats as B spikes this time.

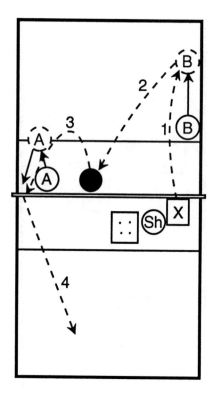

GAME ACTION DRILLS

84 TWO TO THREE-FOUR VERSUS TWO-FIVE DEFENSE, TRANSITION, AND ATTACK DRILL

Objective: To train tip coverage and transition to attack.

Description: The drill begins with the coach tossing the ball and players A and B transitioning from their base positions. The coach mixes up spikes and tips to the center front (#3) and left front (#4) positions. Both players move to play the spiked or tipped ball. The appropriate player should play the ball to the setter. Player A then transitions to spike. The setter back sets to player A in the right front (#2) position. Player A approaches and attacks, and the drill continues.

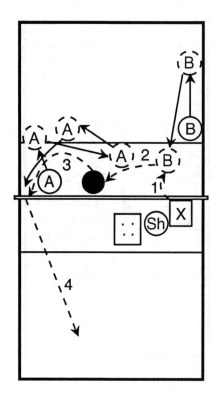

85 TWO TO TWO-FIVE LIVE DEFENSE, TRANSITION, AND ATTACK DRILL

Objective: To train defense, transition, and attack against an actual spiked ball.

Description: The drill begins with the coach tossing the ball to Player C who approaches and spikes to either player A or B. As shown in the diagram, player C elected to spike to player B who digs to the setter in the target area. Once the ball is spiked to player B, player A prepares to spike. The setter back sets to player A in the right front (#2) position. Player A approaches and spikes to a specific area. The coach tosses another ball and the drill continues.

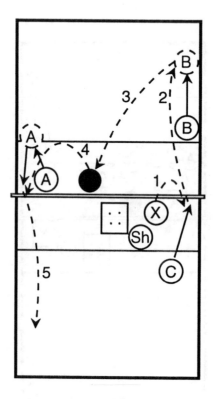

86 TWO TO TWO-FIVE NON-STOP TRANSITION AND ATTACK DRILL

Objective: To train game action dig, transition, and attack skills.

Description: The drill begins with the coach tossing the ball to the setter. The setter sets the ball to player C. Both players A and B transition from their starting positions to their new defensive positions and prepare to dig. Player C approaches and spikes the ball down the line to player B. Player B digs the ball to the setter on the same side of the net. Player A transitions to attack. The setter back sets the ball to player A who approaches and spikes to player D. Player D digs the ball to the setter and the drill continues. In the second sequence, player D should spike cross-court to player B and player A should spike cross-court to player C.

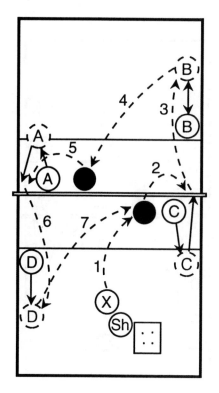

87 TWO TO TWO-FIVE NON-STOP DRILL WITH BLOCKER

Objective: To teach digging around the block while continuing to train dig, transition, and attack skills.

Description: The drill begins with the coach tossing the ball to the setter. The setter back sets the ball to player C. Both players A and B transition from their starting position to a new defensive position and prepare to dig. Player C approaches and spikes the ball past player F toward player B. Player B digs the ball to the target area, and the setter prepares to back set. Player A transitions to attack, and the setter back sets to the right front (#2) position. Player A approaches and spikes the ball down the line, past player E who is blocking, to player D. Player D digs the ball to the target area, and the drill continues with player C approaching and spiking past the block cross-court to player A, alternating the direction of the spike and the digger.

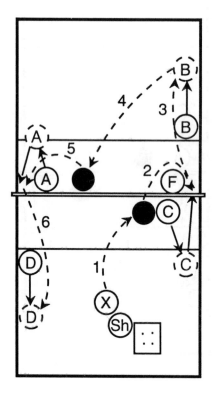

88 TWO TO TWO-FIVE NON-STOP DRILL WITH BLOCKER AND PENETRATING SETTER

Objective: To teach digging around the block while continuing to train dig, transition, and attack skills.

Description: The drill begins with the coach tossing the ball to the penetrating setter. The setter back sets the ball to player C. Both players A and B transition from their starting position to new defensive positions and prepare to dig. Player C approaches and spikes the ball past player F toward player B. Player B digs the ball to the target area, and the setter prepares to back set. Player A transitions to attack, and the setter back sets to the right front (#2) position. Player A approaches and spikes the ball down the line past player E who is blocking to player D. Player D digs the ball to the target area. Player C approaches and now spikes the ball past the block cross-court to player A, alternating the direction of the spike and the digger.

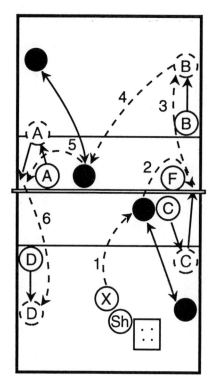

CHAPTER 4

ADDITIONAL DEFENSIVE DRILLS

89 DIG-SET-SPIKE DRILL

Objective: To train the skills of digging and executing an offense from a dig.

Description: The coach hits to player A. Player A passes to a penetrating setter. The setter sets to player B. Player B spikes anywhere in the court. After 10 good spikes, the players rotate positions.

Variations:

1. Change the position of the defense.

2. Change the coach's position.

3. Change the position of the hitters.

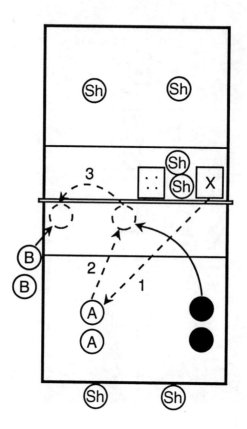

GAME ACTION DRILLS

90 EVER-READY DEFENSE DRILL

Objective: To develop the skills involved in readiness on defense and digging a cross-court spike.

Description: The drill involves having two players on one side of the court, located near the sidelines. The coach initiates the drill by tossing the ball to the setter. The setter then alternates setting to the two attacking lines, C and D, while the hitters spike near the cross-court diggers, players A and B. Each pair works for two minutes and changes sides after one minute.

Variation: Have the diggers assume a position on the sideline and work on defending against a down-the-line attack.

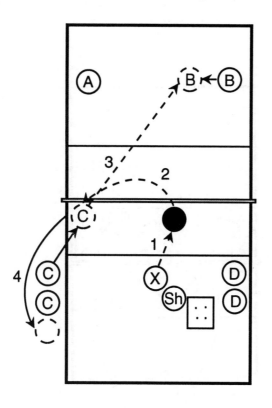

91 TWO PLAYER COMPLEX TRAINING DRILL

Objective: To master the combined skills of digging, setting, and spiking in actual game situations.

Description: Players A and B start in the left back (#5) and right back (#1) positions on the court. There are two coaches located on the opposite side of the net in the right and left front (#2 and #4) positions. The coach in the #4 position spikes to player A. Player A digs the ball to player B. Player B penetrates to set the ball to player A for a spike. The sequence is then repeated from the other side.

Variations:

1. Coaches spike down the line and run the same drill.

2. Vary the height, speed, and position of the set.

3. The coaches act as blockers when the set is positioned outside.

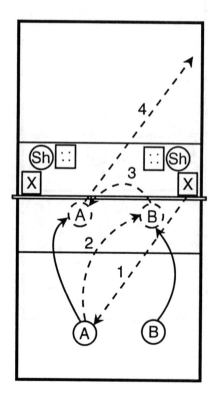

92 DEEP SET VOLLEY DRILL

Objective: To learn to attack the opponent's right back (#1) position on a broken play.

Description: The coach begins the drill by tossing to player A. Player A passes to the setter. The setter sets to the attack line. Player B spikes the ball toward the right back (#1) position of the opponent's court. Player C plays the ball to the setter who sets to the attack line. Player D spikes the ball toward position #1 of the opponent's court, and the drill continues. Set a goal for a specific number of volleys without a miss.

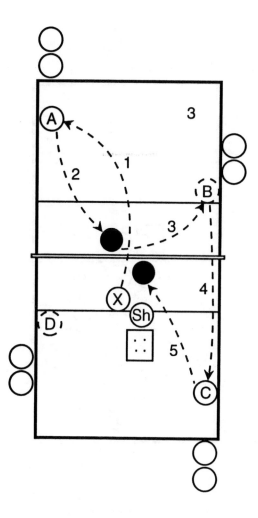

93 THREE PLAYER DEFENSE DRILL

Objective: To practice backcourt defense.

Description: The coach stands in the middle of the court, close to the net. Diggers play in the left back (#5) position, the center back (#6) position, and the right back (#1) position, according to their strengths. The coach hits to any of the three positions. If player A or B digs the ball, then player C will set to the coach. If player C digs, player A will set to the coach.

Variation: The coach hits from the right or left front position.

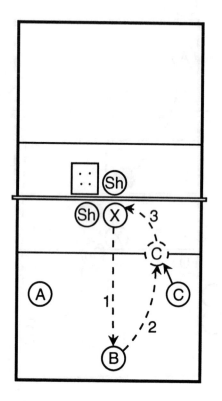

GAME ACTION DRILLS

94 FOUR TO FOUR-FIVE-SIX DRILL

Objective: To develop backcourt defense and transition to attack.

Description: The coach starts the drill by spiking to either player A, B, or C. In the diagram, it is shown that player C digs the first spike to the setter, and player A transitions off to spike. The setter sets the ball outside. Player A approaches and spikes the ball.

Variation: The drill may be performed from the right front (#2) position.

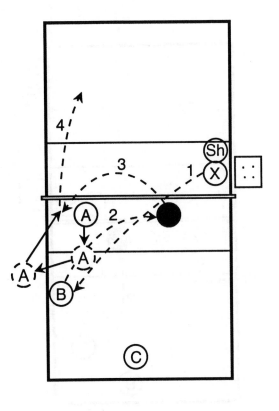

95 FOUR TO ONE-SIX-FOUR DRILL

Objective: To develop defensive positioning in the backcourt and transition to attack.

Description: The coach spikes the ball to either player A, B, or C. In the diagram, player A transitions off the net after the spike. Player C digs the ball to the setter, and player A transitions off to spike. The setter sets outside, and player A hits down the line. If player B digs the ball, the setter transitions out to spike, and player C comes in to set the ball to either player A or the setter.

Variation: The coach may spike from the opposite side.

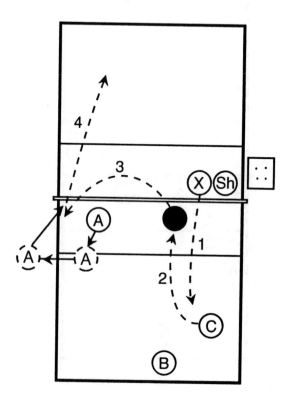

96 FOUR TO ONE-SIX-FIVE LIVE DRILL

Objective: To develop defensive positioning around a one-player block. To improve outside blocking techniques.

Description: The coach tosses/sets at fairly rapid intervals. After spiking one ball, the players in line A rotate clockwise. The blockers (players marked "B") rotate after three attempts. The defensive players (C, D, and E) position themselves around player B and attempt to touch every ball spiked or tipped. After two minutes, the players are rotated: hitters to blockers, blockers to defenders, defenders to shaggers, and shaggers to hitters.

Variations:

1. Have the blockers and hitters move either to the middle or the right side.

2. Have the coach toss the ball to a setter.

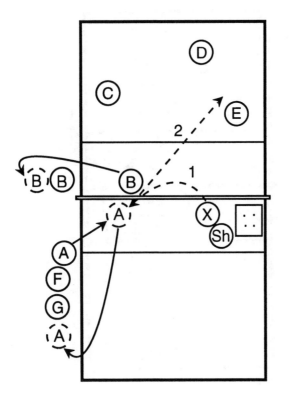

97 FOUR TO ONE-SIX-FIVE VARIATION DRILL

Objective: To work on three player backcourt defense, setting, and spiking a set from an angle.

Description: The coach tosses to either player A or B. The player passes the ball high to the other receiver. This receiver sets to player C. The three diggers work to pass the ball spiked by player C. Players can stay in the same position for several rounds, or they can rotate to a new position each attack.

Variations:

1. Run the same drill using a weak side attack.

2. Add blockers.

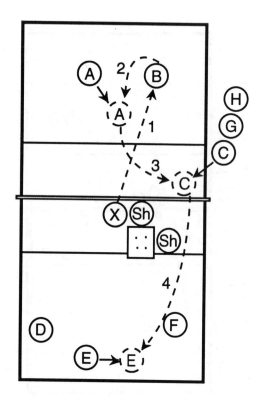

98 FOUR TO FOUR-FIVE-SIX NON-STOP DRILL

Objective: To develop ball control and teamwork in the backcourt.

Description: The coach starts the drill by tossing a ball to the setter. The ball is set outside after player A transitions. Player A spikes the ball to either player D, E, or F. The ball is dug to the setter, and player D transitions off to spike. The setter sets to player D. Player D spikes the ball to the left front (#4), left back(#5), or middle back (#6) position player on the opposite side, and the drill continues.

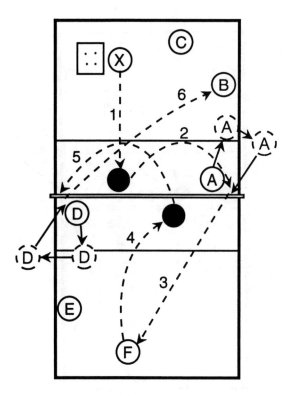

99 FOUR TO ONE-SIX-FOUR NON-STOP DRILL

Objective: To improve ball control and defensive positioning.

Description: The coach tosses the ball to a setter. Player A transitions to spike. The ball is set outside, and player D transitions off the net for defense. Then player A spikes to either player E or player D. In the diagram, player E digs the ball to the setter, and player D transitions out for the spike. The ball is set outside, and the drill is repeated.

Variation: The setters may also block prior to setting.

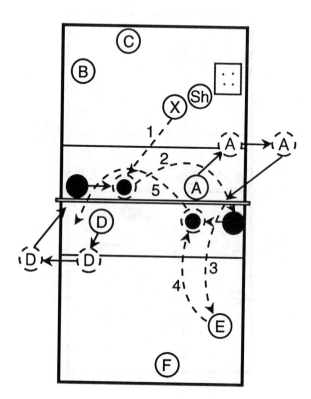

GAME ACTION DRILLS

100 FOUR TO ONE-SIX-FIVE-FOUR DRILL

Objective: To develop teamwork and positioning for backcourt defense.

Description: The coach slaps the ball to indicate that player D should transition off for defense. The coach may spike the ball to any of the backcourt players. In the diagram, The coach spikes and player B digs the ball to the setter. Player D transitions off to spike as the setter comes off the block to set. The ball is set outside. The spiker approaches and hits.

Variations:

1. The coach can spike from the right front (#2) position, making player D the blocker.

2. The coach could spike from the middle front (#3) position.

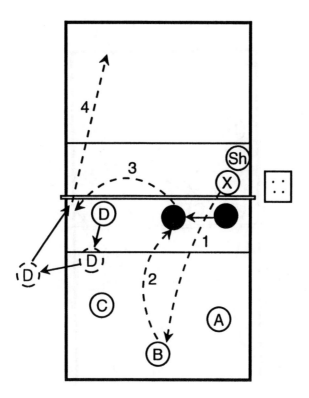

101 HIT AND "D" DRILL

Objective: To develop the offense's ability to hit around the block. To improve defensive teamwork, specifically digging around the block.

Description: The coach tosses the balls continuously to player A. Player A tries to hit around players B and C forming a two player block to score. The defense tries to block or dig each hit then transitions and attacks. As illustrated below, player D digs to the target area. Player B, after landing from blocking, transitions to set. Players C and G transition to spike. Player B sets to player G, and player G approaches and spikes. After six balls have been successfully blocked or dug by the defensive group and kept in play, the two groups switch sides of the net.

Variations:

1. Omit the block or use only one blocker.

2. Have the hitters move to either the middle or the right side.

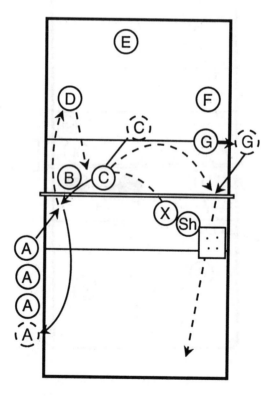

GAME ACTION DRILLS

102 DEFENSE-TO-OFFENSE CONVERSION DRILL

Objective: To practice digging, improve teamwork, and develop transition to attack.

Description: The coach tosses to the setter. The setter sets to either A, B, or C. The hitter spikes, and the defense on the opposite side tries to dig and counter-attack. Substitute four new players after the defense has successfully run 10 counter-attacks.

Variations:

1. Run combinations sets to the hitters.

2. Have the setter try to block the counter-attack.

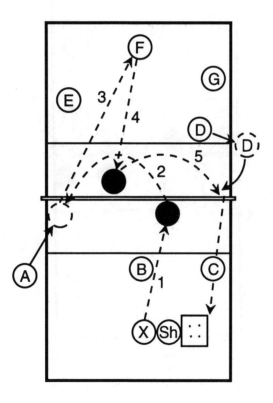

103 FOUR TO ONE-SIX-FIVE-FOUR NON-STOP DRILL

Objective: To develop ball control and team defense.

Description: The coach starts the drill by tossing a ball to the setter. Player A transitions off to spike, and the ball is set outside. Player E transitions off the net for defense. The ball can be spiked to either player E, F, G, or H. In the diagram below, player G digs to the setter as player E transitions off to spike. The ball is set outside, and the drill continues.

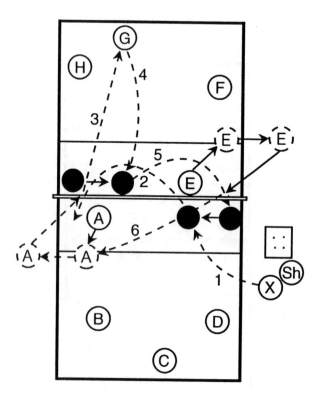

104 TEAM PEPPER DRILL

Objective: To work on defensive positioning, team communication, team ball control, and conditioning.

Description: The setter located in the center front (#3) position sets a high ball to either player A or G. The ball is spiked with control at one of the defenders. As shown below, player E digs the ball to the center front setter. The setter sets to either player F or B. Run the drill for two minutes before players rotate positions.

Variation: All players can play all positions, or they can play their specialized position.

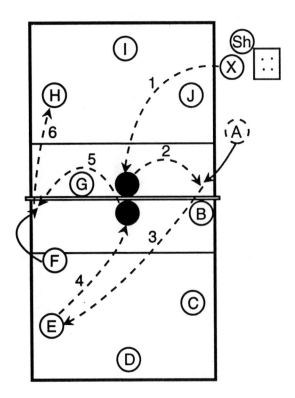

CHAPTER 5

SERVE AND DIG TRANSITION DRILLS

105 SERVE TO DIG POSITION ONE DRILL

Objective: To train serving, positioning for defense, and to practice spike reception.

Description: Player A serves and then transitions for defense. The coach spikes to player A. Player A passes to the target area.

Variation: The coach may spike from the left front (#4), middle front (#3), or right front (#2) position.

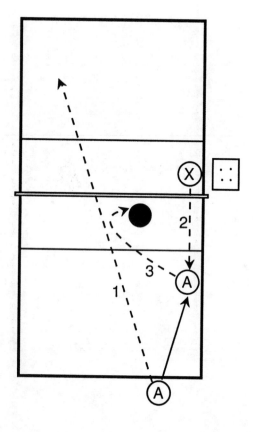

106 SERVE TO DIG POSITION SIX DRILL

Objective: To train serving, positioning for defense, and to practice spike reception.

Description: Player A serves and then transitions to defense positioning. The coach spikes to player A, who passes to the target area.

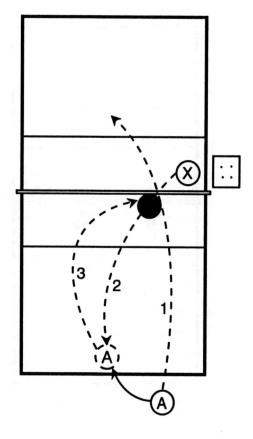

107 SERVE TO DIG POSITION FIVE DRILL

Objective: To train serving, defense positioning, and spike reception skills.

Description: Player A serves and transitions to defense positioning. The coach spikes to player A. Player A passes to the target area.

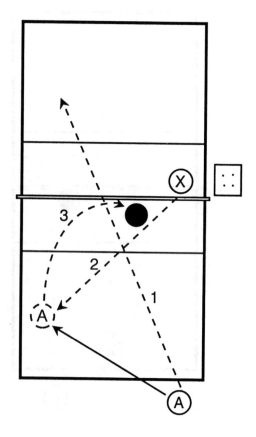

108 SERVE TO DIG POSITION SIX LIVE DRILL

Objective: To train the transition from serve to defense, and to practice digging accuracy.

Description: Player A serves and transitions for defense. The coach tosses a ball to player B. Player B spikes to player A. Player A passes to the target area.

Variations:

1. The server may transition to the left back (#5), middle back (#6), or right back (#1) position.

2. The spiker may be in the left front (#2), middle front (#3), or left front (#4) position.

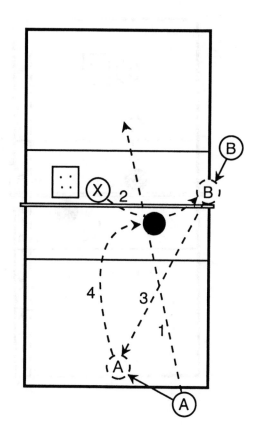

109 SERVE TO DIG POSITION ONE LIVE PROGRESSION DRILL

Objective: To train serve to defense transition and digging accuracy.

Description: Player A serves and transitions to play defense. The coach tosses another ball to a setter. The setter sets to player B. Player B spikes to player A, who passes to the target area.

Variations:

1. The digger may be in the right back (#1), middle back (#6), or left back (#5) position.

2. The spiker may be in the left front (#4), middle front (#3), or right front (#2) position.

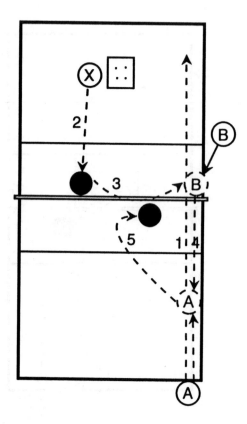

110 SERVE TO DIG DRILL WITH BLOCKER

Objective: To train serve to defense transition. To train defense position around a block.

Description: Player A serves and transitions for defense. The coach tosses a ball to player B. Player B attempts to spike the ball past a blocker to player A. Player A passes to the target area. If the spike is blocked, the drill is stopped.

Variations:

1. The server may transition to the left back (#5), middle back (#6), or right back (#1) position.

2. The spiker may attack from the left front (#4), middle front (#3), or right front (#2) position.

3. Another blocker may be added.

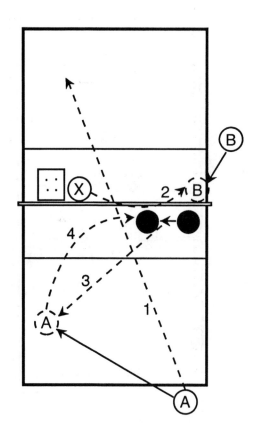

111 SERVE TO DIG WITH BLOCKER LIVE DRILL

Objective: To train serve to defense transition. To practice defense positioning around a block.

Description: Player A serves and transitions to play defense. The coach tosses another ball to the setter. The setter sets to player B. Player B attempts to spike the ball past the blocker to player A. Player A passes to the target area.

Variations:

1. The server may transition to the left back (#5), middle back (#6), or right back (#1) position.

2. The spiker may attack from the left front (#4), middle front (#3), or right front (#2) position.

3. Another blocker may be added.

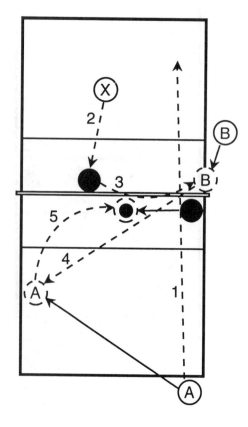

112 SERVE TO DIG LIVE DRILL WITH RECEIVER

Objective: To train the serve and dig sequence, serving, serve receiving, and spiking.

Description: Player A serves to player B, then transitions for defense. Player B passes to the setter. The setter back sets to player C. Player C hits down the line to player A. If player B's pass is not accurate, the coach tosses a ball to the setter to keep the drill going.

Variations:

1. Have the server play different defense positions.

2. Vary the position of the receiver or spiker.

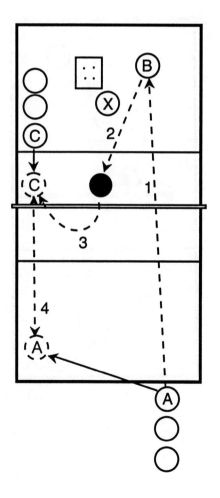

113 SERVE TO DIG TIP DRILL

Objective: To train ball control and server's switch.

Description: Player A serves to player B, then transitions for defense. Player B passes to the setter. The setter sets a quick ball to player C. Player C tips to the opponent's left front (#4) position. Player A must play the ball to the target area.

Variations:

1. Have the front row passer receive and attack from different positions.

2. Have the server play different defense positions.

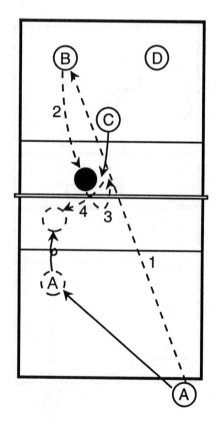

GAME ACTION DRILLS

114 SERVE TO TWO PLAYER DEFENSE AND TRANSITION DRILL

Objective: To train defensive positioning and teamwork. To practice the transition from defense to offense.

Description: Player A serves, and both player A and player B transition for defense. The coach spikes a ball to either player. The player digs the ball to the target area. Player B transitions out to attack. The coach tosses a ball to player B for a spike.

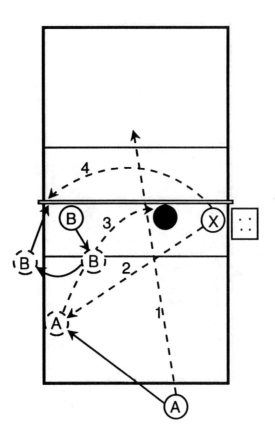

115 SERVE TO TWO PLAYER DEFENSE AND TRANSITION DRILL

Objective: To train defensive positioning and teamwork. To practice transition from defense to offense.

Description: Player A serves, and both player A and player B transition for defense. The coach spikes a ball to either player. The player digs the ball to the target area. Player B transitions out to attack. The coach tosses a ball to player B for a spike.

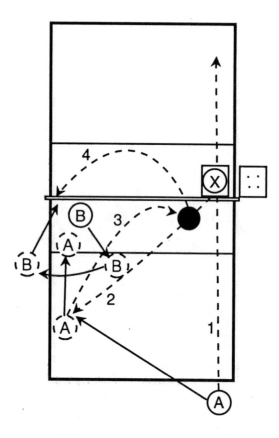

116 SERVE TO TWO PLAYER DEFENSE AND TRANSITION PROGRESSION DRILL

Objective: To train defensive positioning and teamwork. To practice transition from defense to offense.

Description: Player A serves the ball, and players A and B transition off for defense. The coach spikes a ball from a stand to A or B. The player digs the ball to the setter, and player B transitions out to attack. The ball is set outside, and player B spikes as A covers the spiker.

Variation: One or two blockers may be added to the drill.

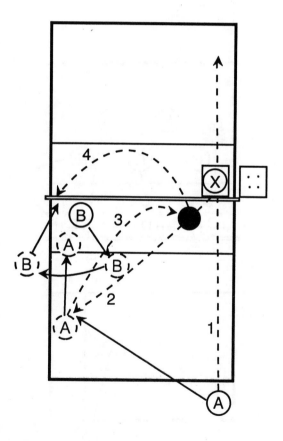

117 MONSTER "D" DRILL

Objective: To develop full service reception and attack, attack serve, and individual defense.

Description: One side lines up in their usual service reception formation. They will pass, serve, and attack, using all their play sequences. The players are instructed to serve every ball for an ace and will receive two points for each ace and lose one point for an error. Player A then becomes the only digger, the "monster". Player A is awarded one point for touching the ball, two points for playing the ball up, and three points for playing the ball above the level of the net inside the attack line. The side that gets fifteen points first is the winning team.

Variation: Change the players' positions on the court and require attackers to spike in a specific direction.

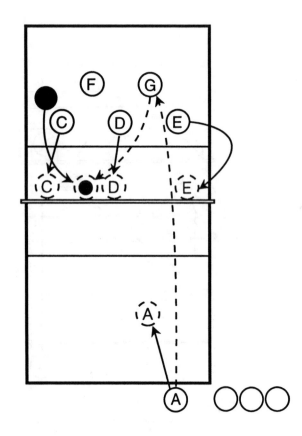

GAME ACTION DRILLS

118 SERVE-RECEIVE AND DEFENSE DOUBLES DRILL

Objective: To work on team serve reception and attack. To challenge two players on defense.

Description: The group is divided into two teams — one receives while the other serves and plays defense. The pair receives one point if either player can play the ball after it has been spiked or tipped by the receiving team. The receiving team scores when the ball is played for a kill and is not touched by either defender. The receiving team should try to run the options off the serve receive they use in a game. the first team scoring five points wins, and the teams switch sides.

Variations:

1. Any ball touched by the defenders earns a point.

2. Use three defenders.

3. Allow the defenders to counter-attack so that the receiving team works on transition.

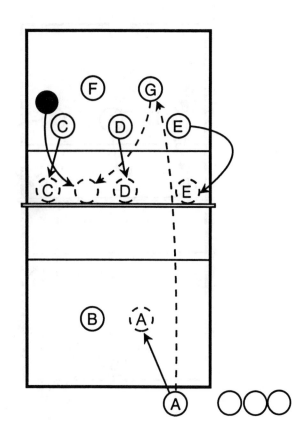

119 SERVE-RECEIVE AND DEFENSE TRIPLES DRILL

Objective: To work on team serve reception and attack. To challenge three players on defense.

Description: The group is divided into two teams — one receives while the other serves and plays defense. Player A serves and joins players B and C on the court for defense. The defense receives one point if any player can play the ball after it has been spiked or tipped by the receiving team. The receiving team scores when the ball is played for a kill and is not touched by any defender. The receiving team should try to run the options off the serve receive they use in a game. The first team scoring five points wins, and the teams switch sides.

Variations:

1. Any ball touched by the defenders earns a point.

2. Allow the defenders to counter-attack so that the receiving team works on transition.

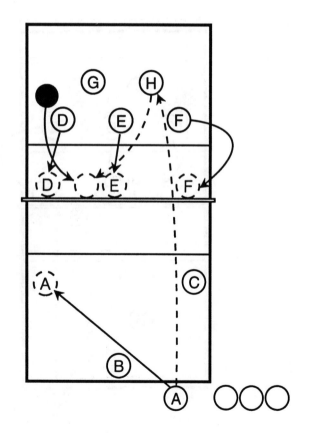

GAME ACTION DRILLS

120 SERVE-RECEIVE AND DEFENSE TRIPLES DRILL WITH A BLOCK

Objective: To work on team serve reception and attack. To challenge three players on defense, working with a blocker.

Description: The group is divided into two teams — one receives while the other serves and plays defense. Player A serves and joins players B and C on the court for defense. The defense receives one point if any player can play the ball after it has been spiked or tipped by the receiving team. The receiving team scores when the ball is played for a kill and is not touched by any defender. The receiving team should try to run the options off the serve receive they use in a game. The first team scoring five points wins, and the teams switch sides.

Variations:

1. Any ball touched by the defenders earns a point.

2. Allow the defenders to counter-attack so that the receiving team works on transition.

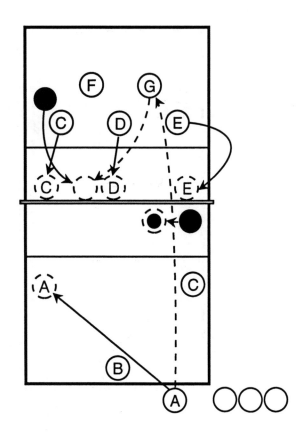

CHAPTER 6
RECEIVE AND ATTACK
TRANSITION DRILLS

121 SERVE, PASS, AND SET DRILL

Objective: To work on serving, passing, and setting.

Description: Player A serves to player B. Player B passes the ball to the setter. The setter sets to player C. Player C catches the ball and returns it to player D. Player D gives the ball to player E. Rotate from server to receiver, from receiver to setter, from setter to catcher, from catcher to shagger, from shagger to server.

Variation: Start the receivers at the attack line and serve deep. This requires the receivers to move backwards before passing.

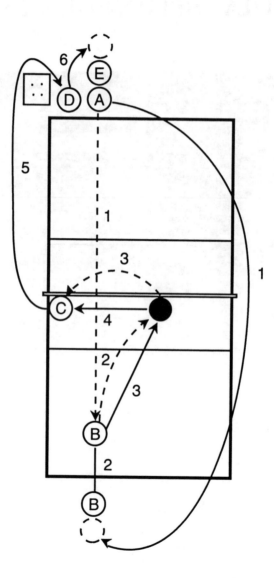

122 COMBINATION PASS, SET, SPIKE, AND COVER DRILL

Objective: To work on passing and setting accuracy. To develop spiking and spiker coverage.

Description: The coach serves to player A. Player A passes to the setter. The setter sets a high ball to player B. Player A and the setter move in to cover player B. Player B spikes the ball, retrieves the ball, and goes to the end of the shagging line. Other players rotate by following the path of the ball.

Variations:

1. Vary the position of the receiving and spiking lines.

2. Vary the type and difficulty of the serves.

3. Add blockers, or have someone toss a ball for spiker coverage.

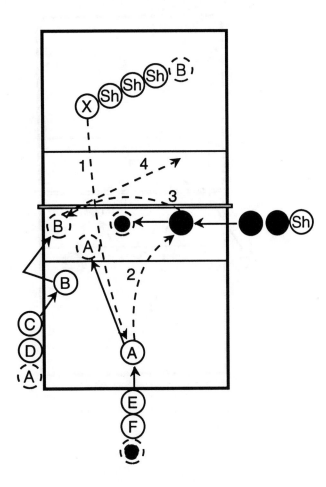

123 DEEP-TIP COMBINATION DRILL

Objective: To work ball control in serving, passing, setting, and tipping.

Description: Player A serves to player B in the left back (#5) position. Player B passes to a penetrating setter. The setter sets to player C. Player C tips to the opponent's right back (#1) position. The drill is repeated until a prescribed number of successful executions are completed. Rotate clockwise.

Variations:

1. Tip cross-court.

2. Add blockers.

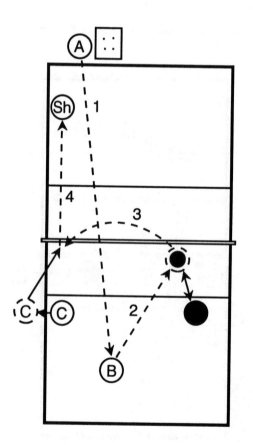

124 BEAT-THE-BALL DRILL

Objective: To develop concentration, ball control, and accuracy in serving, receiving, setting, and spiking.

Description: Balls are served by players A and B at the same time, directly to players C and D. The passes must go to the setters with minimum movement of the setters' feet. The setters set the hit back to players A and B, taking no more than two steps to retrieve the hits. Each successful execution earns one point for the players. Each unsuccessful play earns one point for the ball. The ball starts out with ten points, and the players start with zero points. The object is for the players to reach fifteen points before the ball does.

Variation: Change the players' positions on the court.

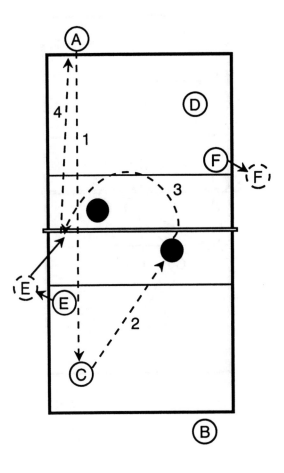

125 INSIDE OUT DRILL

Objective: To train serve-receive teamwork and attack transition.

Description: The coach serves a ball to player A in the left back (#5) position. Player A passes to the setter. The setter set to player C. Player C spikes a cut-back shot. Quickly, the coach tosses a second ball to player B in the right back (#1) position. Player B passes to the setter. The setter sets a high ball to player C. Player C must recover from the first attack, get outside, and hit deep cross-court. The drill is repeated with the coach serving to player B.

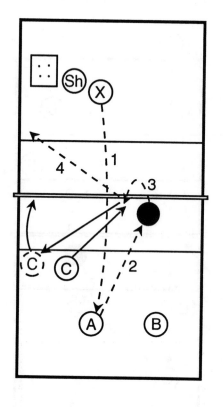

126 SERVE WITH TWO-PLAYER RECEIVE-AND-ATTACK DRILL

Objective: To develop serving and passing skills, team work, and opening up and supporting during serve reception.

Description: Player A serves to player B. Player B calls for the ball and passes to the setter. Player C backs up the play. The setter sets to player D. Player D approaches, jumps, and spikes the ball to the server, player E. Player E serves to player C, and the sequence is repeated.

Variations:

1. The coach calls cross-court or line serves.

2. The spiker moves to the middle or right front position.

3. Add blockers and diggers into the rotation.

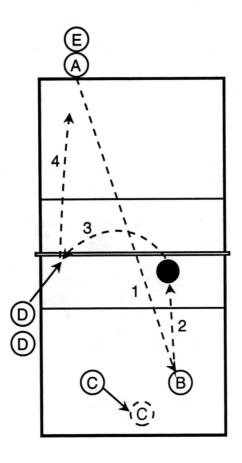

127 ONE-ON-ONE SERVE RECEIVE DRILL

Objective: To develop serving and passing accuracy. To practice transition from receiving to spiking in the right front (#2) position.

Description: Player A serves five balls, one to each receiving position. As soon as player B passes to the setter, the next ball is served. When player B reaches the last position, the setter back sets to player B in the right front (#2) position. After spiking, the player goes to the end of the serving line. Player C quickly moves to the next receiving position. Player D becomes the next server. After serving, player A moves to the receiving line.

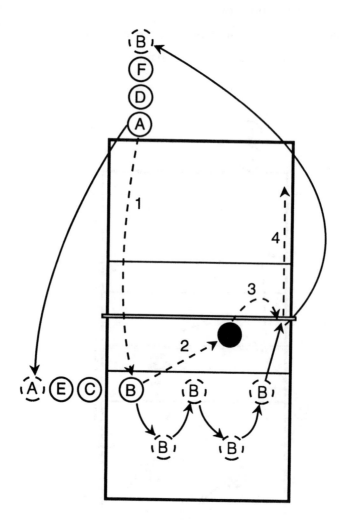

128 PASS AND ATTACK DRILL

Objective: To develop the ability to serve-receive and attack.

Description: The drill begins by player A serving down the line to player B. Player B passes the ball to the coach. The coach sets a high ball or tosses another ball to player B to spike. The drill continues.

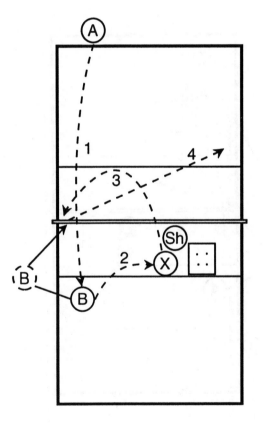

129 PASS AND ATTACK DRILL WITH SETTER

Objective: To train serve reception skills while developing transitional movements for attack.

Description: The coach serves an easy ball to player A. Player A passes the ball toward the setter, and the setter sets the ball for player A to hit. Continue the drill for a specified period of time or a pre-determined goal.

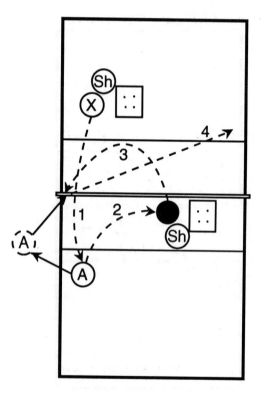

130 PASS AND BACK ATTACK DRILL WITH SETTER

Objective: To train serve reception skills while developing transitional movements for attack.

Description: The coach serves to player A. Player A passes the ball toward the setter, and the setter back sets the ball for player A. Player A approaches and spikes.

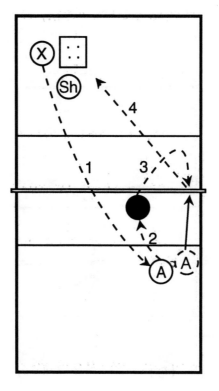

131 PASS AND ATTACK DRILL WITH PENETRATING SETTER

Objective: To train serve reception deep on the court and transition to attack skills. To practice penetrating and setting.

Description: The server (A) serves the ball down the line toward player A. At the same time the ball is being served, the setter penetrates to the right front (#2) position, anticipating B's pass. The setter sets a high ball outside to player B. Player B approaches and spikes.

Variations:

1. Player B can receive anywhere on the court and attack.

2. Vary the position of the sets.

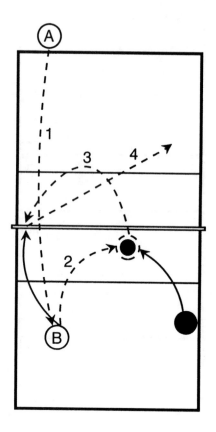

132 TRANS-COMBO DRILL

Objective: To develop quick transition and movement patterns after executing a combination of skills.

Description: Player A serves to player B. Player B passes to the setter. Player B now becomes a hitter, and the ball is set. Player B attacks against players C and D. As players C and D descend, the coach tosses a ball into the net. Player C (the middle blocker) retrieves the ball and plays it up to player E. Player E sets a fast attack to player C.

Variations:

1. Position the receiver in different spots on the court and have the attack at different positions at the net.

2. Have the coach toss the ball into the net so that the outside blockers have to play it.

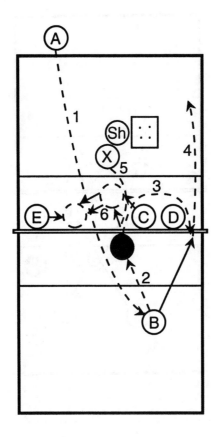

133 QUICK ATTACK DRILL

Objective: To train setting and two-player combinations from serve reception.

Description: The coach serves to either player A or B. The setter penetrates and sets a specific combination depending on who passed the ball. If player A passes, B goes for a quick set, and player A goes for a middle set (2) three to five feet above the net and in front of the setter. If player B passes, player A goes for a half shoot (3), and B goes for a middle set (2) three to five feet above the net. Continue the drill for a specific time limit or a specific number of successful executions.

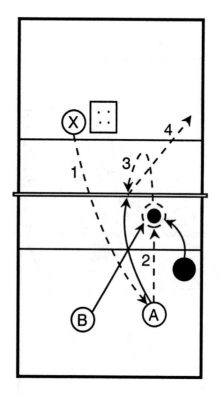

134 ATTACK AND COVER DRILL

Objective: To practice pass, set, and spike sequence. To work on spiker coverage with resulting counter-attack.

Description: The coach serves to players A and B. The player that receives the serve passes to the setter, and the ball is set outside to left front (#4) position. Player C spikes against players D and E standing on tables. The ball is deflected into the hitter's court, and players A and B cover and attempt a counter-attack. After five times, rotate from blockers to shaggers, shaggers to passers, passers to hitters, and hitters to blockers.

Variation: Use the setter as a participant in spiker coverage.

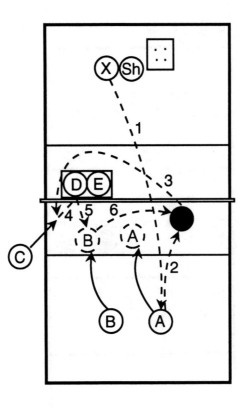

135 THREE PLAYER SERVE RECEIVE AND ATTACK DRILL

Objective: To concentrate and perfect team serve reception fundamentals while giving all players the opportunity to pass, set, hit, and serve.

Description: Divide the team into groups of five players. On each side of the net, one player serves (D), one sets, and three receive (A, B, and C). Players A, B, and C must successfully pass a ball to the setter. The setter sets to either player A or C for a hit. After ten successful passes, sets, and hits, the players rotate to new positions.

Variations:

1. Run the same drill without the setting and hitting if more concentration on passing is desired.

2. Vary the position of the receivers.

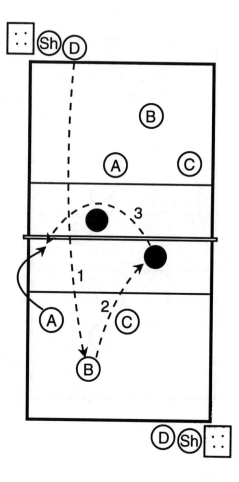

136 FORTY-NINTH PARALLEL ATTACK DRILL

Objective: To develop the techniques involved in movement and passing, setting various sets, calling play sets, and running particular combinations.

Description: The drill is initiated by having player B serve the ball to player A in the middle back (#6) position. Player A passes the ball to the setter, regardless of where it is served. The setter works with three spikers, players C, D, and E. (**Note:** Teams that run particular plays should work on them in the drill.) After the ball is spiked, the hitter in the right front (#2) position shags it, returns it to the ball cart, and goes to the end of the spiking line. The spiking line rotates to the right after every play.

Variations:

1. Conduct five to ten consecutive attack patterns before switching any players.

2. Immediately replace the hitter who spikes the ball after it has been retrieved.

3. Incorporate two receivers in the drill for passing and spiker coverage.

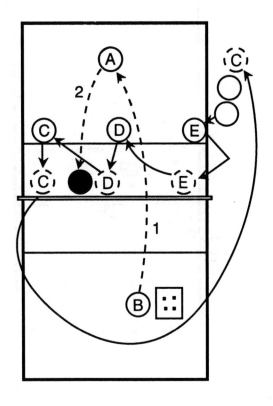

137 SERVE TO THREE AND ATTACK DRILL

Objective: To work on serve receiving, setting, and spiking. To develop serve placement.

Description: Three receivers, players A, B, and C, line up in a triangle, simulating the three center players of a W formation. Player B must serve six balls, two to each position. Players A, B, and C attempt to pass to a setter positioned at the net. The setter sets to player E in the left front (#4) position. After each group completes its turn, the players rotate.

Variations:

1. Vary the receivers' position.

2. Vary the position of the attackers.

3. Have the server assume defense position.

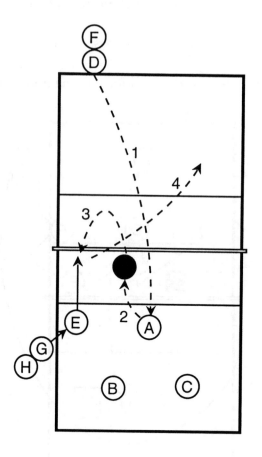

138 THREE PLAYER COMPLEX TRAINING DRILL

Objective: To master the combination attack after service receptions, with spiker coverage and transition to blocking.

Description: Three players A, B, and C line up in the court for service reception, and one server (player D) stands in the opponent's service area. Player D serves to one of the three players, (player C in this example). Player A should be the setter moving near the net. The two remaining players, B and C, will be spikers. When player B spikes, the other two players move in for spiker coverage. After the spike, all three players move to block in the right front (#2) position where the coach is located to spike.

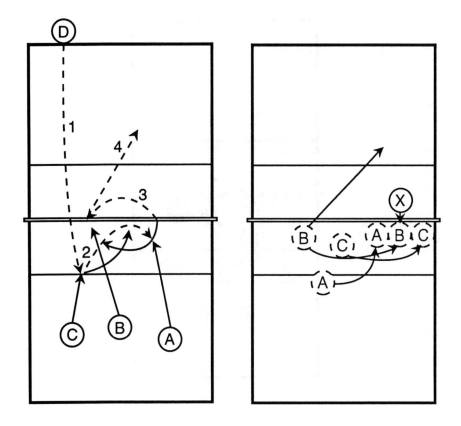

139 COMBINATION PLAY-DECISION DRILL

Objective: Players set up in a W serve-reception formation. The setter selects one of two plays involving the left front (#4) position player (A) and the middle front (#3) position player (B). If player B receives the serve, then run a play requiring player A to move first. If anyone other than player B receives the serve, player B moves first.

Variations:

1. Have the setter use different play sets, requiring the non-passing player in the front row to run the faster pattern.

2. Use three front row players in the combination.

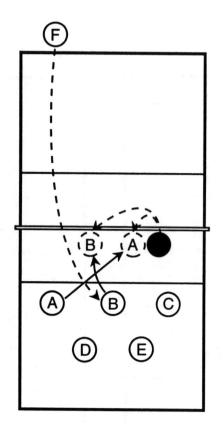

140 LOSERS PAY DRILL

Objective: To practice serve reception formations, passing accuracy, and play sets.

Description: Designate a serve reception formation and play set. The team must accurately execute passes and attacks with no errors. The ball starts with ten points and the team with zero. Each time the team passes and attacks successfully, the ball loses one point and the team gains one point. Play to fifteen points. If the ball wins, players must perform exercises that are specified for the loser.

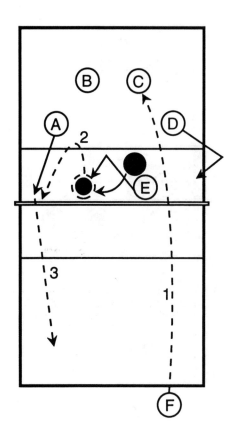

141 BOX COVERAGE DRILL

Objective: To concentrate on watching hitter and opposition's block on coverage. To practice converting a blocked ball into an offensive play.

Description: The coach serves or tosses a ball to the receiving team. The receiving team passes, sets, and hits into the block. Spiker coverage passes the ball and converts to an attack. The ball is blocked again. Try to keep the sequence going as long as possible.

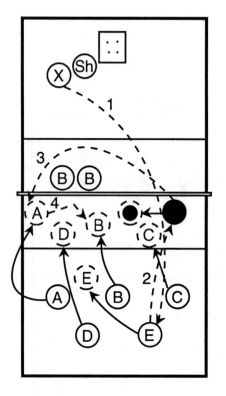

142 THREE-THREE-THREE DRILL

Objective: Varies depending on the needs of the team. Areas of emphasis can be team blocking, serve reception, attack combinations, free ball execution, and spiker coverage.

Description: Divide the team into three groups of three, each group consisting of a setter/offsetter, outside hitter, and middle blocker. One group blocks (B), one groups attacks (A), and one groups passes (C). The coach sets to one of the three attackers. The blocking groups tries to stop the hitter. Depending on the area of concentration, set the goal of ten balls to be successfully blocked, spiked, or passed.

Variations:

1. Vary the coach's position and type of serve or toss.

2. Use different attack combinations.

3. Vary serve reception patterns.

4. Add a serving group.

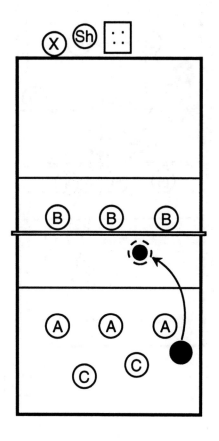

143 MULTIPLE OFFENSE HITTING AND BLOCKING DRILL

Objective: To practice team attack and play sets from serve reception positions. To work on blocking combinations.

Description: Player A alternates serving to the right back (#1) position and the left back (#5) position. The first receiver, player B, passes from position #1, and a play is run. Then, player C passes from position 5, and another play is run. Blockers should work together, reading and calling switches as the play demands. Continue the drill until a specific number of successful plays are executed.

Variation: Have the setter penetrate from each of the three back court positions as well as the front court, using a five-one system.

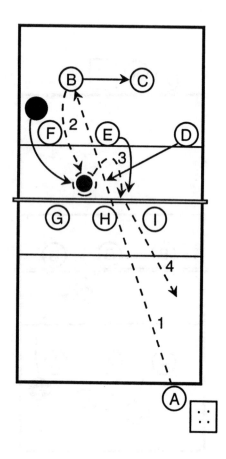

144 ENDURANCE BLOCKING DRILL

Objective: To work on individual blocking skills, positioning, and endurance. To continue development of team serve reception and attack.

Description: The coach serves to player D. Player D passes to the setter. The setter sets to any of the three hitters. The blocker, player F, must react to the set and move to block. As soon as the hitter (in this case, player C) has landed, the next pass has already been made to the setter, so the drill moves rapidly. After the blocker blocks ten balls, a shagger becomes the new blocker. The hitters rotate one position to the right, and another shagger becomes a hitter.

Variation: Have two blockers working together.

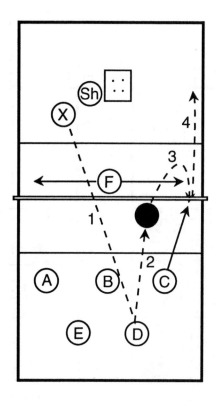

145 CUBAN COVERAGE DRILL

Objective: To learn proper spiker coverage from service reception and transition.

Description: The server, player A, serves to any area on the court. The setter penetrates, and the receiver, player B, passes to the setter. The setter sets to any of the three hitters on the court. In this diagram, player E receives the serve. The receiving team covers accordingly. Player E spikes the ball, and the coach tosses a ball over to the covering teammates. The team tries to play the ball up so that the setter can run the offense again. The drill can be continuous.

Variation: After the receiving team passes the ball and the hitter spikes, the coach yells, "Bump, Set, Spike!" The players run to their defensive positions. The coach spikes the ball into the court, and the defense plays the ball up to the setter. The setter runs the offense. The hitter spikes the ball (the rest of the team covers), and the coach tosses the ball over so that the team (coverage) can play the ball up again to the setter.

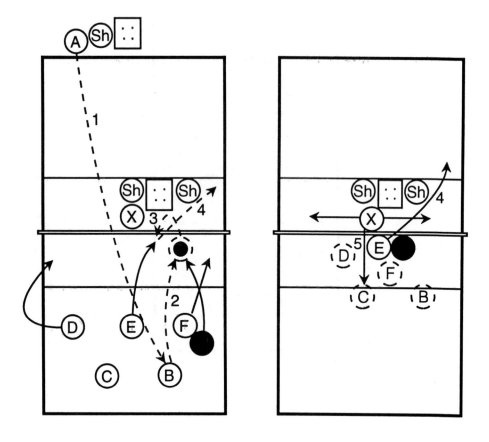

CHAPTER 7

SPIKE VERSUS BLOCK DRILLS

146 ONE ON ONE BLOCKING DRILL

Objective: To teach proper blocking technique and timing.

Description: Players in the A line stand behind the attack line with a ball. On the opposite side of the net, positioned across from line A, is a blocker line (B). The A players self-toss, approach, and spike. The B players position, time, and execute a block. The A players begin by spiking directly at line B but progress to spiking around the blocker.

Variation: Have the A and B lines alternate spiking and blocking each time.

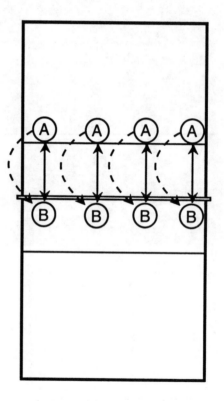

147 ASSIGNMENT BLOCKING DRILL

Objective: To teach a blocker in a one-on-one situation how to control location of a spiker's hit. To teach proper body and hand positioning.

Description: Player A passes to the setter. The setter sets outside to player A for a cross-court attack. Player B must stop this hit.

Variations:

1. Change the hitter's assignment to a line hit.

2. Add diggers (especially to cover the open shot), allowing the spiker to hit any direction.

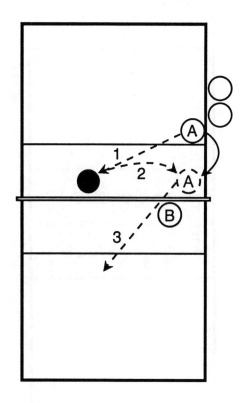

148 THREE PLAYER TECHNIQUE BLOCKING DRILL

Objective: To work on blocking techniques during one-on-one situations and double blocks. To train the off blocker's movement from the net to the defense position.

Description: Player A spikes cross-court. Player B practices the one-on-one blocking technique. Player C spikes the power angle. Player D blocks one-on-one. Player F tries to hit past the block. During the third spike, player B should come off the net for a sharp angle hit or dink. The same three steps are performed again, this time beginning with player F.

Variation: Add defenders.

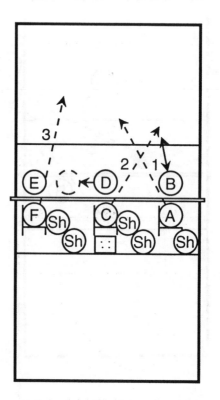

GAME ACTION DRILLS

149 THREE POSITION BLOCKING DRILL

Objective: To develop proper blocking technique and footwork.

Description: Three hitters (A, B, and C) stand behind the attack line with a ball. On the opposite side of the net, positioned across from A, is a blocker (D) prepared to block. A self-tosses, approaches, and spikes. As soon as player D lands, player B self- tosses, and D positions across from player B. Again, as soon as D lands, player C self-tosses. Once player D blocks against all three hitters, D returns to the end of the line, and the next blocker positions across from player A.

Variations:

1. The hitters can increase the rate at which they spike which forces the blockers to move into position to block more quickly.

2. The hitters can change the height and depth of the toss to increase the difficulty in timing the block.

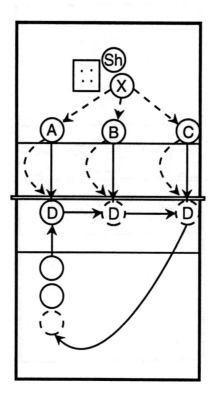

150 PEPPER BLOCK DRILL

Objective: To develop blocking technique and timing.

Description: Players A, B, and C are at the net, approximately five to six feet apart. On the opposite side of the net are two hitters with balls. Each hitter self-tosses and spikes a ball alternately between two blockers, who try to form a two-player block. The hitters alternate spiking.

Variations:

1. Increase the intensity and speed of the hits, forcing the pressure on the blockers.

2. All the hitters try to hit around the block, teaching correct position of the block.

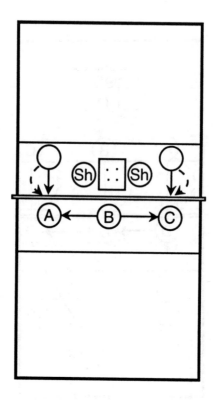

151 BLOCK AGAINST THE OUTSIDE HIT DRILL

Objective: To practice the techniques involved in having outside hitters work against blockers. To develop the skills involved in positioning for an outside block and setting high outside.

Description: The drill is initiated by having the coach toss or bounce a ball to the setter. The setter then penetrates and sets high outside to player A. Player A attacks against players B and C. The drill continues until a predetermined number of successful hits/blocks has been achieved.

Variation:

1. Have the setter assume a position in the center court.

2. Have the hitters and blockers work from both sides of the net.

3. Have a second hitter call out the open shot to the first hitter.

4. Incorporate a digger in the drill.

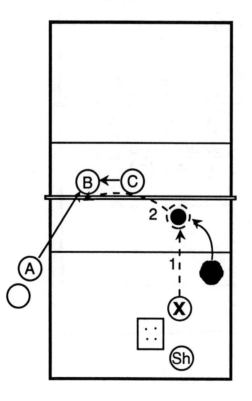

152 BLOCK AND RECOVER DRILL

Objective: To train the middle blocker in the movement patterns and mechanics of blocking. To teach blockers transition for tip coverage.

Description: The coach tosses a ball over the net, simulating an over-bump, for player A to block. The coach quickly tosses another ball to the setter, who sets a high ball to player B. Players A and C position to block. Player B tips over and three feet behind player A, who must tip the ball up to the target.

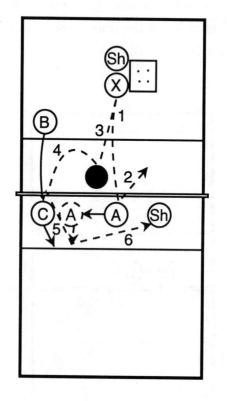

153 BLOCK TWO DRILL

Objective: To train double block communication and movement. To develop attack transition and swing hitting.

Description: The coach tosses a ball to the setter. The setter sets a high ball to player A. Player A tries to spike through or around players B and C. Immediately after the spike, the coach tosses another ball to the setter. The setter sets to the right front (#2) position. Player A sprints to position #2 to spike. Players B and C quickly move into position to try to block. Repeat the same sequence with Player D. Continue for a set time limit or a specific number of successful blocks.

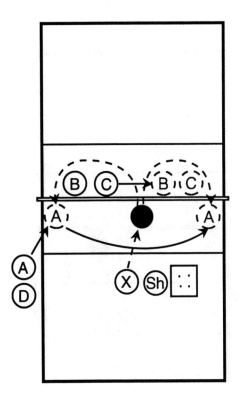

154 THREE TRIPS DRILL

Objective: To practice setting and hitting from different positions. To work on transition in attacking and individual and team blocking.

Description: The coach tosses three balls to the setter. The setters sets the first ball to the left front (#4) position, the second to the center front (#3) position, and the third to the right front (#2) position. Player A spikes from position #4, backs off, approaches for a quick set in the middle, backs off, and approaches for a spike from position #2. Player A then returns to the end of the hitting line. Players B, C, and D either block or back up to play defense, depending on the position of the hitter. After each hitter has gone through the sequence three times, groups rotate.

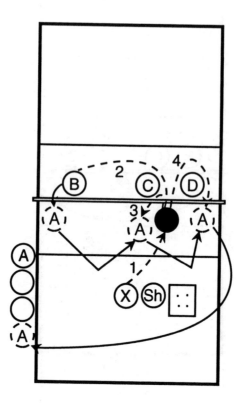

GAME ACTION DRILLS

155 TEAM BLOCKING

Objective: To develop the skills involved in setting from various positions and under various conditions. To enable hitters and blockers to practice adjusting to sets from various positions on the court.

Description: The drill begins by having the coach stand at center court and toss balls to the setter at the net. The coach varies the tosses to different positions on the court. The setter must set every tossed ball. The hitters (A, B, and C) and blockers (D, E, and F) must adjust to the tosses and the sets. The coach tosses the next ball as soon as a hitter spikes. Emphasize forming a good team block.

Variations:

1. Have the setters move initially from behind one of the hitting lines, and use more than one setter.

2. The coach may assume a position on the other side of the net and toss balls to players. The players must then pass the tossed ball.

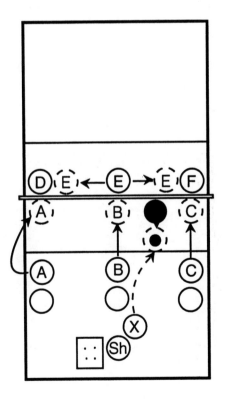

CHAPTER 8

ATTACK & BLOCK TRANSITION DRILLS

156 BLOCK TRANSITION SPIKE DRILL

Objective: To teach transition from blocking to spiking. To train blocking form and spiking skill.

Description: Player A mock-blocks and transitions off the net. The coach tosses a ball outside. The player approaches and spikes.

Variations: Drill may be done for middle front (#3) and right front (#2) positions too.

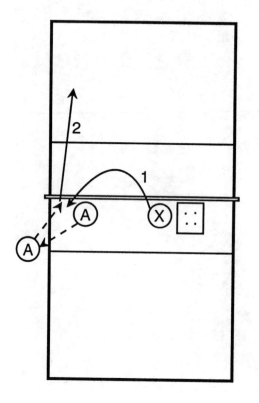

157 BLOCK TRANSITION SPIKE DRILL WITH SETTER

Objective: To train transition from blocking to spiking. To train blocking form and spiking skill.

Description: Player A mock-blocks and transitions off the net. The coach tosses the ball to a setter. The setter sets the ball outside, and player A approaches and spikes.

Variation: The spiker could be in any of the front row positions.

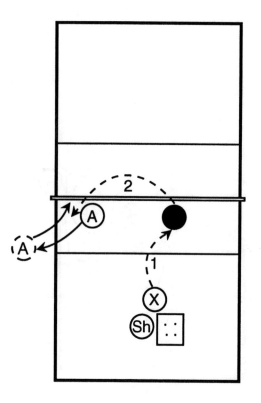

158 BLOCK TRANSITION ATTACK DRILL

Objective: To improve blocking technique and transition from blocking to attacking.

Description: Player A, standing on a stand, spikes the ball. The right front (#2) player (B) tries to block the spiked ball. If successful block occurs, the drill stops. If the ball is not blocked, player B will transition off to attack. The coach will toss a ball to the setter. The ball is set outside, and player B approaches and hits.

Variation: Drill could be run from middle front (#3) and left front (#4) positions.

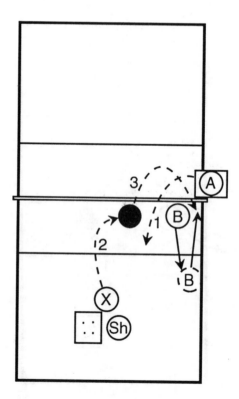

159 BLOCK, DIG, TRANSITION TO ATTACK DRILL

Objective: To improve blocking technique, digging around block skills, and transition from blocking to spiking.

Description: The coach spikes down the line to player A around a block made by player B in the left front (#4) position. Player B transitions outside to attack. Player A digs the ball to a target area. The ball is set to player B, and player A moves in to cover the spike.

Variation: Spiker, digger, and coach may be in the middle front (#3) or right front (#2) positions.

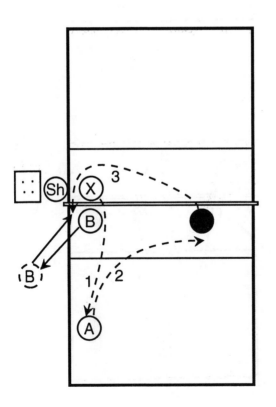

160 BLOCK TO HIT DRILL

Objective: To develop two player block offense and ability to transition.

Description: Two players, A and B, take a blocking position versus a coach on the opposite side of the net. The coach will hit the ball over, around, or off the blockers to player C. Player C digs to the target area, a setter will position to set the ball to either player A or B. Both A and B have quickly transitioned off the net into attack position. The same players should stay in the drill until they have successfully completed a specified number of transition attacks.

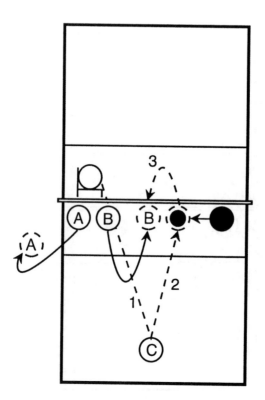

GAME ACTION DRILLS

161 TRANSITION QUICK ATTACK DRILL

Objective: To work on the transition from blocking to a quick attack.

Description: The coach hits at player A while a quick hitter and the setter block. The hitter (B) and the setter (C) turn in the direction of the ball, and player B moves to the net while player C backs off the net. The setter sets quick (one-set) to player C. Make the drill goal-oriented for the hitter.

Variations:

1. Move the digger to the left back (#5) position.

2. Move the coach to the right front (#2) or middle front (#3) position.

3. Add a blocker for more of a challenge.

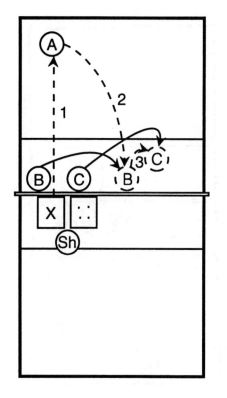

162 SAVE THE SETTER DRILL

Objective: To work on ball control. To practice offense off the transition from defense to offense.

Description: The coach stands on a table and hits past players A and B to player C. The setter penetrates from deep in the right back (#1) position and sets a combination play for players A and B. Immediately after a successful counter-attack, the drill is repeated.

Variations:

1. Spike the ball to the setter, forcing the right front player to set.

2. Run the drill from the opposite side or middle.

3. Add another digger and spike at the seam between them.

4. Vary the offense run on the counter-attack.

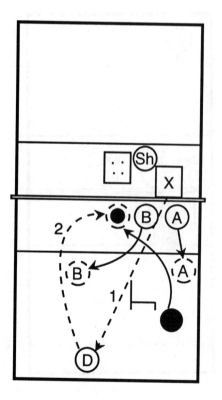

163 KILLER DRILL

Objective: To train block, spike, and dig sequences. To develop endurance.

Description: The drill begins with players A, B, C, and D jumping to block. The players A and C back off the net and spike a toss from the coach on the same side of the net. Players B and D try to stop the hitter across from them, and players E and F try to dig the ball if it gets past the block. Then all players rotate clockwise. The drill continues until every hitter has attempted ten spikes.

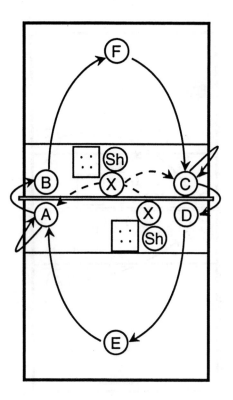

164 FOUR SKILL MOVEMENT DRILL

Objective: To train player movement sequence in four skills.

Description: The coach tosses a ball to player A. Player A sets over the net to player B. Player B passes to player C in the target area. Player C (the setter) then back sets to player B in the right front (#2) position. Player B spikes into the opponent's position #2 past player A's block. Player A receives another ball from the coach, and the drill continues. In the event that player A blocks player B, the drill is continued in the same manner.

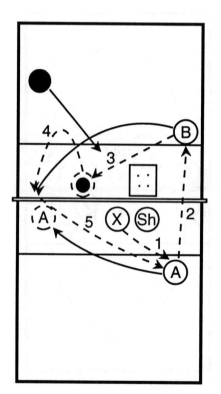

165 ONE HITTER SPIKE AND BLOCK DRILL

Objective: To develop attack transition and team blocking.

Description: The coach tosses a ball to player A. Player A passes to the setter and drives for a middle hit. Player B tries to stop the spike. Player A back-pedals diagonally, receives another ball tossed from the coach, and passes to the setter. The setter sets high outside to player A. Player B joins player C, and they try to block. Hitters and blockers rotate within their respective lines until the coach instructs them to switch sides of the net.

Variation: The coach can be anyplace at the net.

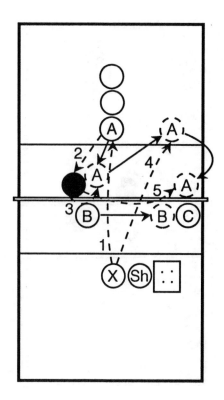

166 CONTINUOUS BLOCK, DIG, TRANSITION TO ATTACK DRILL

Objective: To develop blocking technique, digging around the block, and transition from blocking to spiking.

Description: The coach starts the drill by tossing a ball to the setter on player B's side of the net. The setter back sets to player B. Player B approaches and spikes a controlled hit past player A to player C. Player C digs the ball to C's setter. Player A transitions off the net and prepares for the set. The setter sets to player A. Player A approaches and attempts to spike past player B to player D, and the drill continues. If control is lost or the spiker gets blocked, the coach tosses another ball, and the drill resumes.

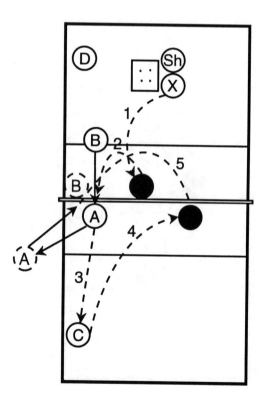

167 BLOCKER TO HITTER TRANSITION DRILL

Objective: To train blockers to make the transition to offense.

Description: Player A tosses the ball to be spiked by player B as player C tries to block. Then player C moves off the net and prepares to hit a tossed ball from player D, and player B prepares to block. This sequence continues until a player has blocked three balls.

Variation: Toss balls to a setter.

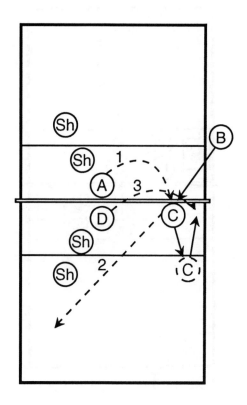

168 MIDDLE BLOCKER TO MIDDLE HITTER TRANSITION DRILL

Objective: To train middle blockers to make the transition to offense after blocking.

Description: The first tosser, player C, tosses a ball to player A. Player A approaches and hits against blocker B. If the block is successful, the drill stops. If player A succeeds, the players switch tasks, and player B transitions off to spike. Player D tosses to player B, and the drill continues.

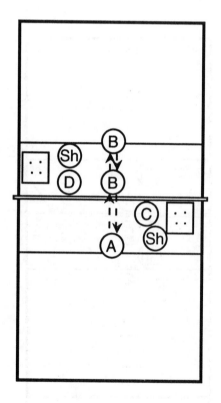

169 MIDDLE BLOCKER TO MIDDLE HITTER TRANSITION DRILL WITH SETTERS

Objective: To train middle blockers to transition quickly from blocking to attacking.

Description: The coach begins the drill by tossing a ball to the setter on B's side. The setter back sets a quick set. Player B approaches while player A moves into position to block. Player B spikes the ball past player A. Player A quickly transitions off the net to prepare to spike. Player A's coach tosses a ball to the setter, and player A immediately approaches to spike. Player B moves into position to block. If player A spikes the ball past player B, the coach will continue the drill by tossing a ball. If player B blocks the ball, the coach tosses in a new ball so the drill is continuous.

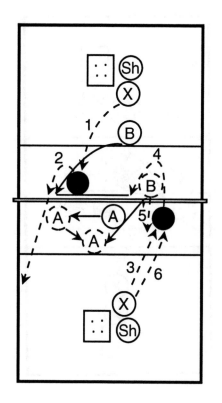

170 ONE VERSUS ONE HITTING AND BLOCKING TRANSITION DRILL

Objective: To work on quick transition from blocking to attacking, and to develop endurance.

Description: The coach tosses a ball to the setter. The setter back sets the ball to player A. Player A approaches and hits against player B's block. If the block is successful, the drill stops. If not, player A stays at the net to block player B. Player B transitions off the net to spike. The drill is repeated but to the opposite side.

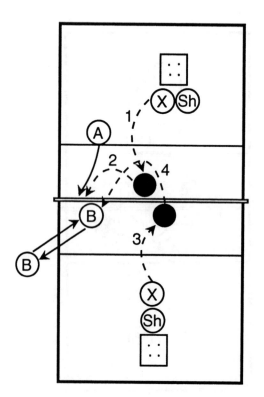

GAME ACTION DRILLS

171   TWO VERSUS TWO HITTING AND BLOCKING TRANSITION DRILL

Objective: To work on quick transition from blocking to attacking, and to develop endurance.

Description: The coach tosses the ball to the setter. The ball is set to player A. The opposing setter and player B try to block the spike. Immediately after the spike, the coach tosses to player B's setter, who sets to player B. Player A and the setter try to block the spike. The drill continues for a specified time or until a team has blocked a certain number of balls.

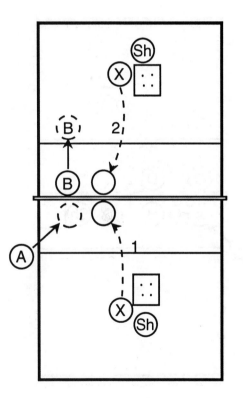

172 BLOCK EXCHANGE DRILL

Objective: To develop double-blocking technique, to give spikers a chance to hit against a double-block, and to develop endurance.

Description: The coach tosses a ball to player A. Player A spikes against the opposing blockers (C and D). After the hit, players A and B exchange positions and get in position to block. Player C backs off the net, and the coach tosses another ball for player C to hit. A and B attempt to block. After the hit, C and D exchange positions, and B backs off the net to hit against the block. Players always exchange positions after their side hits. The drill continues for 25 tosses.

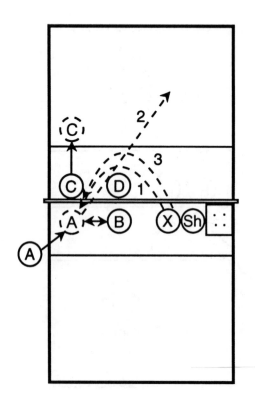

GAME ACTION DRILLS

173 BLOCK EXCHANGE DRILL VARIATION

Objective: To improve transition from blocking to attacking. To develop team blocking skills.

Description: The coach starts the drill by tossing the ball to the setter. The setter back sets to player A. Player A attacks against players C and D. If player A spikes past players C and D, then C and D quickly transition to attack. The setter penetrates, and the coach on their side tosses the ball to the setter. The setter can set to either player. In this diagram, the setter sets to player D, requiring players A and B to move along the net and team block in the middle front (#3) position opposite player D. Player D approaches and spikes, and the drill continues. If the ball gets blocked and covered, the drill continues live. If the ball gets blocked to the floor, the coach on the side the ball was blocked tosses another ball.

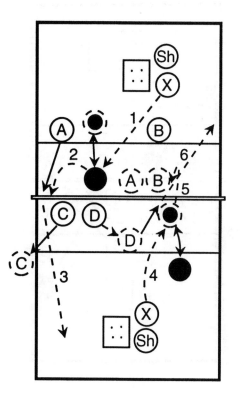

174 FRONT COURT TRANSITION DRILL

Objective: To improve front court transition from offense to defense.

Description: The drill starts by the coach tossing the ball to the setter. The setter sets to player A. Player A hits cross-court past players B and C, who are forming a double block, to player D. Player D plays the ball and gets ready to hit. The setter has two offensive options: to set high outside or to set to player C in the middle front (#3) position. Players D, C, and B will have to spike against players E, F, and A. The drill continues until the ball hits the ground. The coach on the side the ball lands on immediately tosses in another ball to keep the drill going.

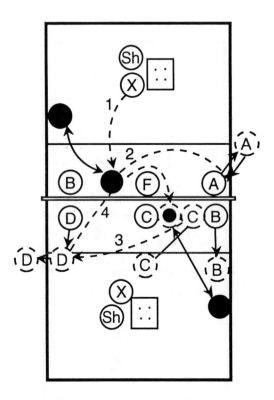

175 ATTACK, TEAM DEFENSE, AND TRANSITION DRILL

Objective: To work on team defense coordination, communication, and court coverage. To practice transition from defense to offense.

Description: The coach tosses a ball to the setter. The setter sets to one of the three hitters, player A, B, or C. These attackers control spiking the ball to insure transition. The defense reacts to the set and assumes defense positions. The defense plays the ball and makes the transition to offense including spiker coverage position. Once the defensive team successfully counter-attacks, the coach immediately tosses in another ball, and the drill continues.

Variations:

1. Include offensive coverage on the hitting side.

2. Call plays for the hitting side.

3. Have the hitters block the defense's counter-attack.

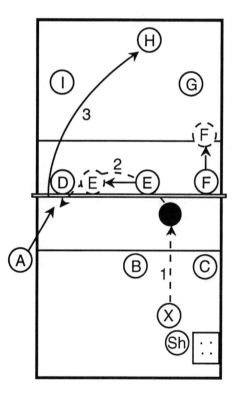

CHAPTER 9

GAME ACTION DRILLS

176 ONE VERSUS ONE DRILL

Objective: To develop ball control and individual skills.

Description: Player A serves the ball and transitions for defense. Player B self-passes, self-sets, and spikes the ball to player A. Player A self-digs, self-sets, and spikes the ball back to player B, and the drill continues.

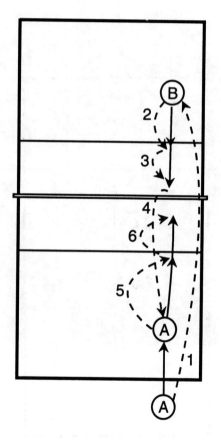

177 ONE VERSUS ONE DRILL WITH COMMON SETTER

Objective: To develop ball control and individual skills.

Description: Player A tosses the ball to the setter. The setter sets the ball and player A approaches. Player A spikes the ball to player B, and the setter goes under the net to set to player B. Player B passes the ball to the setter and approaches to spike. The drill is repeated continuously.

Variation: Two more groups of the same drill can position themselves on either side.

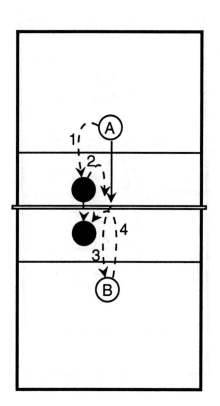

178 THREE PLAYER WEAVE DRILL

Objective: To practice all skills and develop ball control.

Description: Player A tosses the ball to player B. Player B sets the ball to player A and switches positions with player A. Player A hits the ball and goes under the net to set. Player C passes the spiked ball from player A to player A in the target area. Player A sets to player C. Player C approaches to spike. The drill continues with player C spiking to player B.

Variation: This drill may be done by either hitting on the net or hitting from the back row.

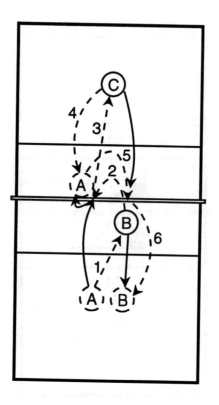

179 TWO VERSUS TWO DRILL

Objective: To achieve skill acquisition during game action. To develop ball control.

Description: The court is divided into three sections by installing two additional antennas on the net as shown. Player A serves to player B. Player B passes the ball to player C. Player C sets for player B to control the spike to player A. Player A digs the ball to player D. Player D sets to player A, and player A spikes the ball to player B. The drill continues.

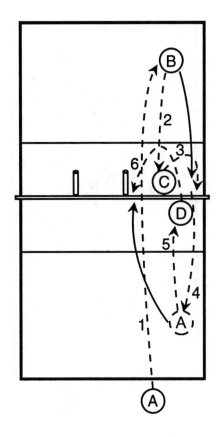

180 TWO VERSUS TWO SWITCHING DRILL

Objective: To develop overall skill work and ball control.

Description: The court is divided into three sections. Player A serves to player B. Player B passes the ball to player C. Player C sets for player B, and player B approaches and spikes a controlled ball to player A. Player B and C switch roles. Player A digs the ball up to player D. Player D sets to player A, and they switch positions. Player A controls a spike to player C, and the drill continues.

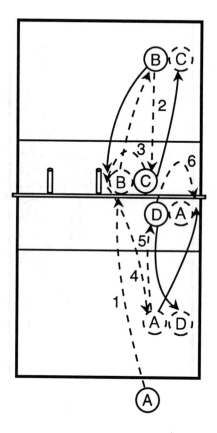

181 TWO VERSUS TWO DRILL WITH BLOCK

Objective: To practice digging around the block, blocking technique, and ball control.

Description: The court is divided into three sections. Player A serves to player B. Player B passes to player C, and player C sets for player B. Player B must spike past player D toward player A. Player A attempts to dig around the block and plays the ball up to player D. Player D sets back to player A. Player C establishes a block, which forces player A to spike in player B's direction, and the drill continues.

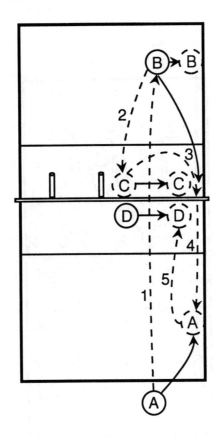

182 TWO VERSUS TWO SWITCHING DRILL WITH BLOCK

Objective: To complete skill training in a game action situation and develop ball control.

Description: As illustrated below, the court is divided into three sections to run three games at the same time. This diagram will show a different sequence on each third to better demonstrate the drill. Player A serves to player B. Player B passes the ball to player C. Player C sets for player B, and player B approaches to spike as player D establishes position to block. Player B spikes past player D toward player A. Player C, after covering player B, switches positions. Player A digs the spike back to player D. Player D recovers from blocking to set to player A, and player A approaches and spikes against player B blocking on the opposite side of the net. Player A spikes past player B toward player C, and the drill continues with players A and D switching positions.

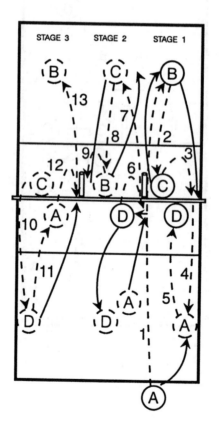

183 CONTROLLED DOUBLES DRILL

Objective: To develop all skills during game play with an emphasis on ball control.

Description: Player A serves the ball over the net to player C and transitions from serving to defense. Player C passes the ball to the center front (#3) position. Player D releases to position #3 to set the ball back to player C. Player C spikes the ball to player A. Player A digs the ball up while player B moves to set the ball back to player A. Player A approaches and spikes to player D, and the drill continues.

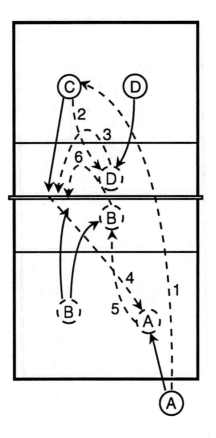

184 DEEP COURT DOUBLES

Objective: To develop all skills during game play with an emphasis on back court spiking.

Description: Player A serves the ball over the net to either player C or D and transitions for defense. Player C passes the ball to the center front (#3) position, and player D releases to set. Player D sets a back court attack to player C. Player D approaches and spikes to players A and B's court. Players A and B defend against player C's spike, and the drill continues.

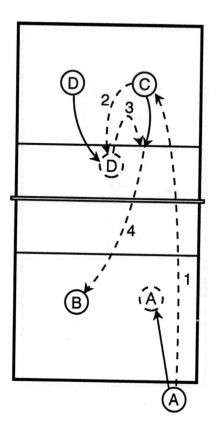

GAME ACTION DRILLS

185 DEEP COURT DOUBLES DRILL WITH COMMON SETTER

Objective: To develop ball control and practice individual skills.

Description: Player A serves a ball over to the opponent's side and transitions off for defense. Player D passes to the setter. The ball can be set to either hitter. In the diagram, the ball is set to player D, and player D attacks. If player B digs the ball, the setter comes under the net, and the drill is repeated.

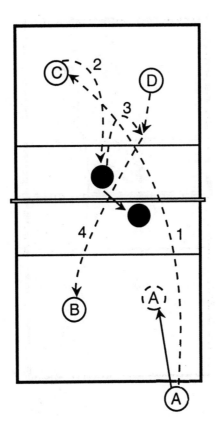

186 FIVE PLAYER WEAVE DRILL

Objective: To develop all skills and ball control during game action.

Description: Player A serves and transitions for defense. Player B passes the ball to the setter. The setter sets the ball to either player C or B in the back row. The player (in this case, B) approaches and attacks, and the setter takes the spiker's position. The spiker goes under the net after the attack and becomes the setter. Player A digs the ball to player B, the new setter. The drill is repeated.

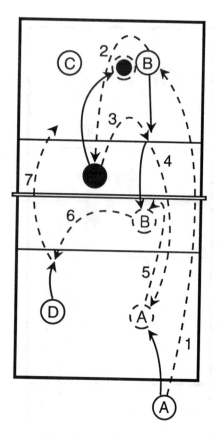

187 BOO-BOO DRILL

Objective: To work on communication, court coverage, and conditioning.

Description: The coach spikes the ball against the floor. The players behind the end line run in, call the ball, and play out the volley against the opposing defense. When the rally ends, the winners become the new defensive team, and the losers go to the sidelines to do any combination of conditioning activities before going to the end of the challenge line.

Variations:

1. Players start by lying face down on the end line.

2. Players start at the net, facing the net. The coach spikes the ball.

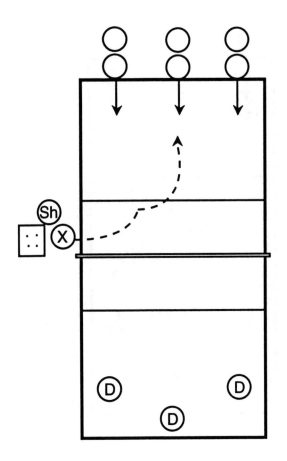

188 THREE VERSUS THREE BALL CONTROL DRILL

Objective: To train ball control and play sequence.

Description: The setter starts by serving to player A. Player A controls the pass to the target area. The setter runs and sets to the left front (#4) position or player B. Player B approaches and hits to player C on the other side. The other side repeats the sequence without stopping the ball. Rotate after completing a specific number of rallies or after a predetermined amount of time. In the event the setter must dig, one of the other players will assume the setting duties for that rally.

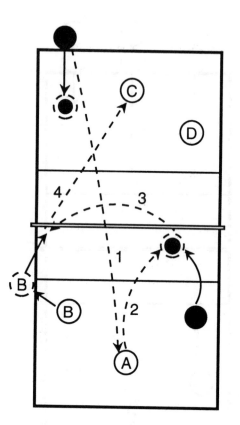

GAME ACTION DRILLS

189 CONTROLLED THREE VERSUS THREE DEEP COURT DRILL

Objective: To improve backcourt defense, transition to offense, and backcourt attack.

Description: Three players are positioned on each side of the net, and their objective is to successfully and successively dig, set, and hit the ball back and forth across the net. With beginning players, ball control should be stressed with the goal to be keeping the ball in play as long as possible. Whenever an error is made, a new ball is introduced at that point to correct the error, and play continues. The coach starts the drill by tossing a ball to player A. Player A passes to the target area where player B will penetrate to set. Player B sets the ball for a backcourt attack by player C. Player C approaches and spikes the ball to player D. Player D digs, and the drill continues.

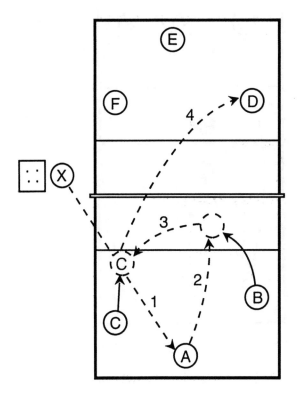

190 THREE VERSUS THREE DEEP COURT DRILL WITH COMMON SETTER

Objective: To improve ball control, backcourt defense and attack, and overall individual skills during game action.

Description: Player A serves the ball and transitions for defense. Player B passes the ball to the setter. The setter sets to any of the three hitters. In this diagram, player C spikes the ball in any direction. The setter goes under the net to set for the other side. The ball is played by player D on the other side of the net. The drill is repeated and continues for a specified number of rallies.

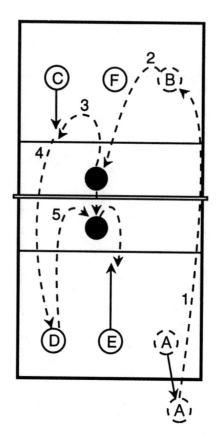

GAME ACTION DRILLS

191 SEVEN PLAYER WEAVE DRILL

Objective: To develop ball control, teamwork, and skill training during game action.

Description: Player A serves and transitions for defense. Player B passes the ball to player C. Player C back sets near the attack line to player D. Player D approaches and spikes to player E, and player C takes player D's (the spiker's) position. Player D, after spiking, becomes the setter for the opponent's side. Player E digs to player D, and then approaches and spikes to player F. Player D replaces player E, and player E is now the setter. The drill continues.

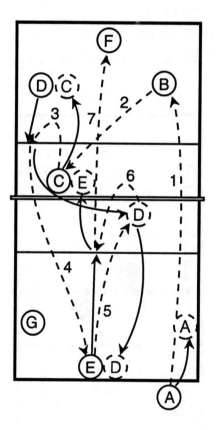

192 FOUR VERSUS FOUR DRILL

Objective: To develop defense, serve, serve receive, setting, and hitting skills.

Description: Player A starts by serving to player B on the other side of the net. Player B passes to the setter. The setter sets to player C. Player C spikes to the defense on the opposite side of the net. Player D digs the ball and passes to the setter on the team. The setter back sets to player E, and the drill continues. After an error, both sides rotate positions. The winning team initiates the next volley with a serve. The serve may go to any receiver, the set to any spiker, and the spike toward any digger.

Variations:

1. Vary the task of the server with deep and short serves.

2. Train backward movement of the receivers by starting them at the three meter line, then serving deep.

3. Start with the setter covering the spiker, then have all players cover.

4. Add the setter as a blocker against the attacker.

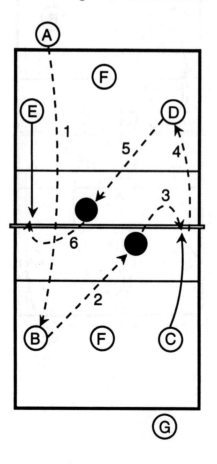

193 FOUR VERSUS FOUR DRILL WITH A COMMON SETTER

Objective: To develop backcourt defense, ball control, and over-all individual skills.

Description: Player A serves and transitions for defense. Player B passes the ball to the setter as player C transitions out for the approach. The setter sets the ball to player C. Player C approaches and hits the ball, and the setter goes under the net to set the ball for the other team. Player D digs the ball to the setter and then transitions out to attack. The setter sets a backcourt attack to player A. Player A spikes the ball, and the drill continues.

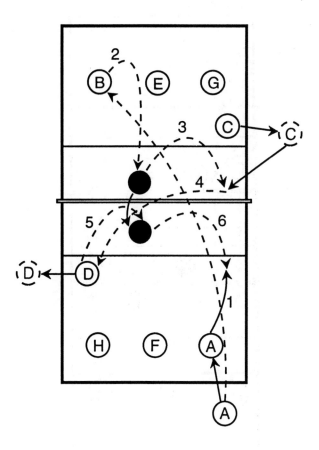

194 NINE PLAYER WEAVE DRILL

Objective: To develop ball control and teamwork during game action.

Description: Player A serves and transitions for defense. Player B passes the ball to player C. Player C back sets near the attack line to player D. Player D approaches and spikes to player A. Player C replaces player D after the spike, and player D becomes the setter on the other side of the net. Player A digs to player D, and player D sets a deep court attack for player A. Player A approaches and spikes to player B, and the drill continues. The blockers are located in the left front (#4) positions so all back sets are deep court against a block, and the only front curt set will be to the player in the left front (#4) position.

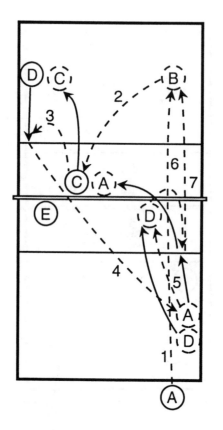

195 FIVE VERSUS FIVE DRILL WITH A COMMON SETTER

Objective: To develop ball control, team work, and team defense.

Description: Player A serves the ball to the opposing team. Player B passes to the setter. Players C and D transition for the attack. The setter sets to any player on the court. If the set goes to the front row players, opponents may set up a single block. Player D approaches and hits to player E. The setter crosses under the net to set for the other team. The drill continues.

Variation: Use your particular service formation or defense system.

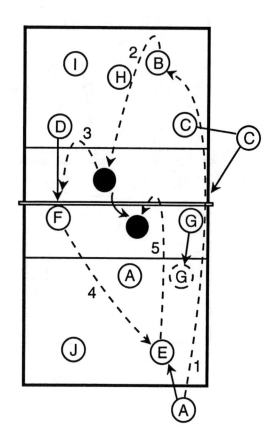

196 ELEVEN PLAYER WEAVE DRILL

Objective: To develop ball control, teamwork, and game action.

Description: Player A serves the ball and transitions for defense. Player B passes the ball to player D. Player E transitions out for an approach. Player D sets the ball to player E in the back court and switches with player E. Player E spikes the ball to the opponent's side and goes under the net to become the setter for the other team. Player A digs the ball to player E, and the drill continues.

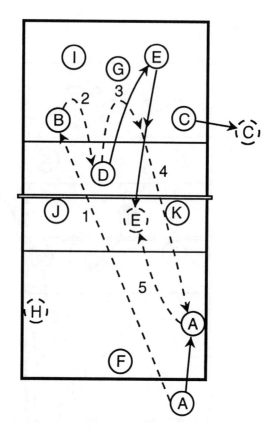

197 DO IT ALL TOGETHER DRILL

Objective: To practice serve reception, offensive plays, defensive formations, and transitions.

Description: The ball is served by player A, and the receiving team (players B, C, D, E, F, and G) passes and runs an offensive play against players H, I, and J. If the ball is successfully attacked, the coach tosses a ball to the setter on the coach's side. The coach's team counter-attacks with an offensive play. Players B, C, D, E, F, and G, now in defensive position, defend against the attack and attempt to counter-attack. The drill continues as long as players B, C, D, E, F, and G defend against the attack and counter-attack. At the coach's discretion, a ball may be tossed to either player K or L on the coach's team to have them pass a free ball or down ball to the receiving team, who must adjust accordingly.

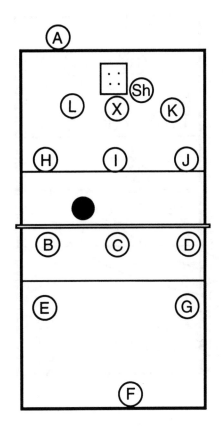

198 ALL-COURT INITIAL MOVEMENT DRILL

Objective: To force initial transition movement. To practice attending and reacting to what the opponent is doing.

Description: Player A serves to the receiving side. The serving team, players A, B, C, D, E, and F, quickly moves to their respective defense positions. The receiving team, players G, H, I, J, K, and L, passes and attacks. If the receiving team immediately ends each play, they receive one point and the serve. If the serving team can keep the ball in play and counter-attack, they receive one point and retain the serve. If either team fails to execute their initial play, they lose a point. Both teams start with fifteen points. The drill continues until one team has lost all their points.

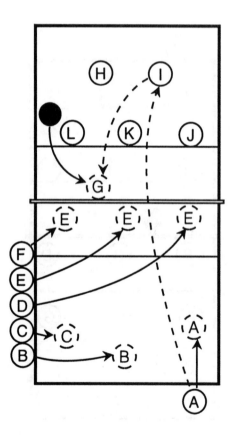

199 SIDE OUT TO SCORE DRILL

Objective: To install the concept of playing to score points after siding out. To maintain intensity while serving.

Description: Player A serves to the opponent's reception formation. Players B, C, D, E, F, and G, the receiving team, attack against no block. Provided that the ball is successfully attacked, the receiving team immediately goes to defense. A ball is tossed by the coach to begin an automatic counter-attack. The play then continues until one side wins the volley. If the receiving team wins, it is a side out, and they can play for one point on the next ball. The ball is tossed to player K on the same side by the coach to initiate the volley. If the receiving team wins the volley, they score a point and are allowed to rotate, and the sequence begins again. The drill is continued until the receiving team scores fifteen points.

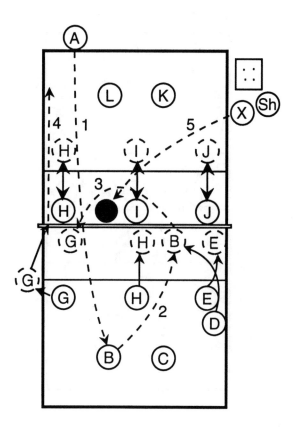

200 SIX PLAYER TIP-DOWN BALL DRILL

Objective: To work on tipping, deep-court spiking, and tip-down ball coverage.

Description: The drill is similar to a full transition scrimmage, except that all balls that are set within the tree meter line must be tipped. The same player may not tip to the same area of the court twice in succession. Any ball deeper than the three-meter line may be attacked and the opposing team plays down defense or regular defense, whichever is appropriate. Each player on the serving side serves two balls until all on the side have served. Repeat the drill with the other side serving. The game is played to fifteen points, scoring one point each time a team wins a volley.

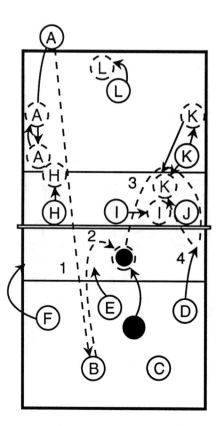

MASTERS PRESS
DIGS VOLLEYBALL!

Volleyball Drill Book: Individual Skills

Bob Bertucci and James A. Peterson, Ph.D.

Written for both players and coaches at all competitive levels, this volume presents drills for developing and improving basic volleyball skills, including serving, setting, spiking, blocking, passing, digging, and service reception. The most comprehensive collection of volleyball drills to date!

$14.95 • paper • 208 pp. • 7 X 10 • illus.
ISBN: 0-94O279-28-2

The AVCA Volleyball Handbook

Edited by Bob Bertucci

Twenty renowned volleyball authorities from around the country have contributed to this first official handbook of the American Volleyball Coaches' Association. Supplemented with charts, diagrams, and photos, this is an essential reference book for both coaches and players.

$17.95 paper • 352 pp. • diagrams, charts, & photos
ISBN: 0-940279-11-8

How to Jump Higher

James A. Peterson and Mary Beth Horodyski

A thorough explanation of how athletes can improve their vertical jump levels by following an organized program of muscular development. Includes information on strength training, plyometric drills, and the use of mental skills such as imagery to develop this crucial motor ability.

$12.95 paper • 144 pp. • drawings & photos
ISBN: 0-940279-12-6

Masters Press books, including all titles in the Spalding Sports Library, are available in bookstores or directly from the publisher by calling 1-800-722-2677.